F. Zell, Richard
Gene

e

Nanon - Die Wirtin vom goldnen Lamm

Komische Oper in drei Akten

F. Zell, Richard
Gene

e

Nanon - Die Wirtin vom goldnen Lamm
Komische Oper in drei Akten

ISBN/EAN: 9783744672320

Hergestellt in Europa, USA, Kanada, Australien, Japan

Cover: Foto ©Thomas Meinert / pixelio.de

Weitere Bücher finden Sie auf **www.hansebooks.com**

"NANON."

A SPLENDID SUCCESS AT THE CASINO.

Monday evening was a grand, red letter night at the Casino. A fashionable audience crammed the beautiful theatre and left scarcely standing room. Crowds of yonng men filled every aisle and the back of the auditorium. The Casino took a new departure on Monday evening under the entire rulership of Messrs. Aronson, who have now the opera management under their control and who were on their trial for the first performance directed by them in conjunction with their coadjutor, Heinrich Conried. The many friends of the Messrs. Aronson, the large number of supporters they have, the habitues of the Casino, to whom it is like a mighty haven of rest and entertainment, as well as large numbers of the lovers of merry music, gathered to help celebrate this all-important first performance.

. . . . . .

"Nanon," the sprightliest opera now on the boards, the musical and literary child of Zell and Genee, Americanized by clever Sydney Rosenfeld, was being given at the Casino with new scenery, gorgeous dresses, handsome appointments and pretty women to boot, and surely it was enough to fill this charming theatre to overflowing.

. . . . . .

"Nanon" is really a delightful operetta, which it took, what the Germans call "geist," to write. The plot is interesting and historical; the characters are picturesque and the situations marked; the music is cleverly written, well instrumented, full of an unnameable swing and rhythm, entirely melodious and as clear to the ear and understanding as a crystal brook. There may be those who sit in judgment on such a work with a wise mind and a corrugated brow, who sagely shake their heads and pick out little black specks in so much brightness and say this and write that, and want to be awfully critical. For them and their show of wisdom "Nanon" was never written or composed; they had better spare their critical faculty for another occasion, for they cannot even understand the motive of "Nanon," the graceful opera "per se," and why should they handle it with their fulsomeness? Zell wrote an exquisite libretto, which Sydney has very nicely adapted—barring some incongruous verses—and which Genee has invested with that kind of rhythmical music that comes from a bright and genial mind and a thoroughly musical temperament. None but a true musician could have written numbers that never jar, are never vulgar, never distasteful to the ear and are connected by a thread of recitative that is melodious of itself. If you want to take "Aida" or "Fidelio" in your pocket to judge "Nanon" by them, you had better not hear "Nanon" at all, for it will remain a myth to you. But if you can descend to be natural once more, enjoy a joke, be charmed with lightness and brightness, take the foam from the cup and be content, then you may judge "Nanon" rightly, understand it and enjoy it; but for goodness sake leave wisdom, critical ability and your encyclopedia at home. "Nanon" needs them not, it is the pure child of the merry fancy of the Viennese school.

. . . . . .

When the curtain rose on Monday last for the first act, there burst upon the crowded audience as pretty a scene as Mazzanovitch alone could paint; quaint, natural and effective. When the curtain rose for the second act the gorgeous and grandiose "Salon" of the old French monarchy expanded before the audience as in a sea of light. Hoyt had in it exhausted his fancy. When the curtain rose for the third act, the picturesque interior of a "Religieuse" loomed up before us; Messrs. Harley and Merry had refined the historical in the description of it. In fact the scenery for "Nanon" was simply superb. The performance began and from the first moment to the last, every one concerned in this joyous operetta did his or her best to be truthful to the conception of Zell and Geneé, to amuse, to carry out in fact the bright fancy of the librettist and composer. If there were faults—and why should there not be?—they were individual; the ensemble was excellent, artistic and thoroughly enjoyable. One could see that some one had been entrusted with the care of the arrangements who had his heart in it and understood the spirit of the operetta, and that was Heinrich Conried.

. . . . . .

The plot of "Nanon" is simple and interesting. A gay cavalier of the court of Louis XIV. falls in love with the beautiful hostess of the Golden Lamb, "Nanon;" but the Cavalier d'Aubigne is a sad love-maker all round, and is also entangled with the lovely Ninon de l'Enclos, the historical beauty of France. Finally he pays court to the lady in supreme power, Madame de Maintenon. There is but a poor look-out for Nanon, who conquers in the end by sheer force of love. D'Aubigne has been losing his time near Nanon, under the disguise of a drummer by name Grignon. Ninon hears of it and comes herself to the Golden Lamb to judge. She is pleased with pretty Nanon, but more pleased still when she hears that Nanon's lover is a drummer, called Grignon; so she promises her protection to Nanon. The marriage day is fixed, the wedding prepared, the guests bring pigs, geese, fowls, cheese, flour, &c., for wedding presents, and d'Aubigne is aghast at the preparations; but before he can sign the contract he is arrested for having fought a duel, the arrest having been brought about by a message to his general, to save him from marriage with the pretty hostess. Nanon is broken-hearted at the loss of her lover. She flies to Ninon to ask for help, for the drummer is sure to be shot or hanged; then confusion becomes stronger, she finds here d'Aubigne, who was naturally set free as a fine nobleman; the idea that she is mistaken in his identity is very charmingly carried out. The king is now to be asked, through Madame Maintenon, to save the drummer's life. Ninon herself goes to Madame de Maintenon to implore her assistance. Nanon follows her, and while waiting in madame's room the king comes in by a private door. Nanon does not know him, but her heart is so full that she tries to gain his interest, does so and obtains a free pardon. With this she rushes away, and only reappears when all the persons concerned are gathered at Madame Maintenon's to find the matter of the supposed drummer is hopeless, and that some one has to forfeit life. Then Nanon runs in with the pardon obtained from the king, and d'Aubigne is so startled by her faithful love that he really offers her his hand, and makes her his countess.

. . . . . .

Through this pretty tale there wanders a curious conceit of the librettist, a song that is invented by D'Aubigne for "Nanon's" Name's day "St. Ann's day." It begins:

"What is this day
That seems to say,"

and ends charmingly.

Nanon in rapture I come to thee,
I come to thee;
Nanon to thee I shall sing for aye,
Yes, shall sing for aye!

The composer has caught the true spirit of the rhythm and has been fortunate enough to set it to so tuneful a melody that it goes of itself. From beginning to end it is the "Leit motif" of love making and winds through the operetta as if Wagner himself had invented it in a happy lightsome mood.

The performance on Monday was a decidedly good and highly amusing one. The gentlemen had the vocal honors thrust upon them; the ladies, besides our favorite comedien, Francis Wilson, bore away the acting honors, and the admixture produced a very happy union. Miss Sadie Martinot as the lovely Nanon was the acme of "chic" and pretty behavior; never overstepping the line. It is not actually necessary for Nanon to be a great vocalist and Miss Martinot managed her limited voice very creditably, at times bringing out her notes with well defined clearness and always singing with agreeable sweetness. That some passages were rather "detoned" or flattened on the first night came solely from the usual nervousness of the first night and will ere this have disappeared. The "vim" with which Miss Martinot carried along the opera and her Cavalier also, was not only delightful, but very useful to Mr. Carleton, whom I have never seen so bright and graceful. He owes great thanks to Miss Martinot that she was not offended at any talk but knew her part must be played with lively brightness or be left alone. She is teaching Mr. Carleton a lesson he needed—that is, to lose his own dignity in the opera in which he performs. He is such a favorite in New York and sings so beautifully those peculiarly sweet numbers, that it will only enhance his value to make him bright and lithesome.

Miss Pauline Hall was at first very stately as Ninon in her fine reception dress, but unbent later; Ninon was in the flesh a woman of such abundant grace that very few people could represent her. Miss Hall acted exceedingly well, but being something of a student of history I find fault with the hairdressing. Ninon was fair and should have had fair hair dressed a la Ninon. Miss Hall has very much improved in singing and need not at all force her higher notes, they are all distinct enough. Her speaking might be a little plainer. The recitative singing of both ladies was remarkably good and showed a careful trainer. As for the hero, Mr. Carleton, why the audience was only too glad to see him back again and listen to those fine baritone notes; he looks somewhat weary, and should not go through the country when New York admires him so much. He must take care of the fatigue in his voice and not exert himself too much; Carleton's voice is the embodiment of those old old English voices of centuries ago, for which some of our best old English songs were written, and he ought to be proud of it. To hear him begin,

"What is the day,"

was a real treat, and he bore himself nobly in the ensembles.

Francis Wilson was more than himself, and if I must speak the truth, he came nearer to a French impersonation, in that black dress of his in the last act; with a little French accent, he could have persuaded one that he was a Frenchman in reality. As for that couplet in the second act,

"To Ninon's glad domain,"

it was excellent. The "boundless glee" was expressed by such pirouetting as Link and Lube could not have improved upon.

roduction of the "Mikado" at the Globe.

eturn of Mme. Judic and Nat Goodwin.

Parisian Romance," "Irish Aristocracy"--Notes.

OLLIS STREET THEATRE—"NANON."

Richard Genée's comic opera of "Nanon" ad its first performance in this city last evening, at the new Hollis Street Theatre, d the attraction, the second presented at is house since its opening, proved sufficient draw together an audience large in point numbers and brilliant in the character of s members. State and city officials occupied e stage boxes, and throughout the audience ould be seen prominent people in all the aried walks of city life. The opera has ade a noted success, both in its original and nglish version, throughout the country; and e Carleton opera company, the organization ppearing last evening, has had the exclusive ontrol of the work in its English form this part of the country. The ook of the opera in its German ersion is an adaptation of a French play ade by Messrs. Zell and Genée, and the bretto used by the Carleton company is a anslation of the German book by Sydney osenfeld. Although the book of the opera as passed through these several hands, retains much of the dramatic interest of the original play, and is articularly strong in its situations and incients. The story of "Nanon" is far from being a fancy sketch, as it deals somewhat freely with many personages and incients in the reign of King Louis XIV. of rance. The argument in detail is as follows: Nanon keeps an inn just outside of Paris alled the Golden Lamb, which has gained enown alike by a casual visit of Louis XIV. and by Nanon's reputation for beauty and virtue. On this account Marsillac, director of the royal theatre, akes his nephew, Hector, an inexperienced country nobleman, to see Nanon. At the ame time the famous beauty, Ninon de Enclos, comes to get a sight of her rival, eing suspicious that her lover, the Marquis 'Aubigné, has turned his affections toward Nanon. She hears that Nanon is going to e married to the drummer Grignan on the ame day, and returns appeased. Grignan s, in fact, the marquis, who, under this isguise, intends to carry off the hostess. he evening before her birthday he, together ith his pretended comrades, a drummer and fifer of the regiment, brings her a serenade. She surprises him with a proposal of marriage, but when the notary, Nanon's relatives and the wedding guests make their appearance, d'Aubigné causes himself to be arrested by his colonel on account of a duel. In the midst of her grief, Nanon receives a ring and compliments from Gaston, the page of Ninon, and she concludes to pray that lady to help her in rescuing Grignan, as by the command of the king duelling is punishable with death. Act 2 passes in the salon of Ninon during a ball. Here come Marsillac, Hector and a gallant abbé, a lover of Ninon and confessor of Mme. de Maintenon, the mistress of Louis XIV. D'Aubigné likewise enters and is joyfully received by Ninon. Reproached for staying away so long and for forgetting her birthday, he draws himself out of his embarrassment by bringing her the serenades which he had already offered Nanon. Nanon comes to ask for Ninon's help in saving Grignan's life; she sees D'Aubigné, whom she thinks she recognizes, but is deceived by his court dress and his distinguished bearing, so that she is persuaded that it is only an extraordinary likeness. Hector and D'Aubigné meet, and the latter, jealous that Hector pays court to Ninon as well as to Nanon, challenges him, and both hurry into Ninon's garden to decide their quarrel by their swords. Meantime, Marsillac, having ... of Grignan, pays homage ... But he is laughed at by Nanon and the company, and D'Aubigné, returning from the duel, is asked to clear up ...

... in the audience room of Maintenon, whose name is also Anna; and to her the abbé sings the drummer's serenade, "Anna, to thee is my dearest way." Marsillac, coming to ask for his nephew's release from prison, obtains the necessary order, chance having betrayed that D'Aubigné, who is a nephew of Main-

NANON.

tenon, gave the challenge. D'Aubigné congratulates her on her birthday with the same "Anna Song," and Marsillac after him, so that the confusion over the origin of the song is renewed. Ninon and Nanon both request audience to pray for grace for their respective lovers, D'Aubigné and Grignan. Nanon receives the life of Grignan as a present from the King, whose favor without her recognizing him she gains so rapidly that he kisses her repeatedly, and she presents the pardon to Ninon in order to save D'Aubigné, in whom she now recognizes Grignan. Touched by so much magnanimity, Grignan offers his hand to her; Maintenon, disquieted by the sudden favor of the King for Nanon, consents, and the hostess of the Golden Lamb becomes the Marchioness D'Aubigné.

The changes incidental to a long continued run of any attraction of this sort have undoubtedly occurred in the lines of the libretto, and so it is difficult to say who is responsible for some of the stupidities of the text. There are, however, fewer of such objectionable features than are usually found after such an extended season of performances as this opera has had by the Carleton company; and it is but just to admit that some of these apparent stupidities struck the audience as particularly funny, thus again showing that what is or is not witty is merely a matter of taste. The management of the beautiful new theatre have shown a wise liberality in putting the opera upon the stage, as a setting has been provided which rivals all former efforts in the staging of a comic opera production in this city. The first act passes in front of the Golden Lamb tavern, which is on the prompt side of the stage, with a quaint overhanging porch to the doorway, which is approached by steps. At the back is seen a view of Paris in the distance, the river Seine winding between the city and the surroundings of the inn. The distance has been managed very cleverly by the scenic artist, and the birches and poplars which go to fill up the scene are "practical," so far as the eye is concerned, their leaves and branches standing out in bold relief against the background. The scene for the second act represents the ball room of Ninon's palace, and here the artistic work of the scene painter is shown in a highly effective way. The general tone of the coloring is a pale-blue and the apartment, with its adjoining halls, stairways and corridors, are brilliantly lighted by stand candelabras at every turn. On the ...

construction, make an elegant st picture, and give an admirable ba ground for the tableaux of the fu An elegant rug upon the floor is keeping with the general character of decoration, and the light streaming in thro the stained glass window gives a warmth a glow to the whole apartment. The bea ornamented architectural features of room are in keeping with the style the times, and the furnishings incl an organ, which is demanded in presentation of the famous waltz song w sung by the abbé. Altogether, the work d by Mr. John A. Thompson, the scenic ar of the theatre, is of the most creditable s and can but add greatly to the attractiven of the opera with the public. The cast gi the opera last evening was as follows:

Nanon Patin.......................Miss Louise E. Pa
Ninon de l'Enclos.......................Miss Alice Vin
Mme. de Maintenon.......................Miss Clara Wi
Gaston, page to Ninon.............Miss Josephine Bart
Marquis de Marsillac.................Mr. Charles H. D
Hector Vicompte de Marsillac..........Mr. C. M. Leum
Abbé.......................Mr. Joseph S. Greensfe
King Louis XIV.......................Mr. Tom G
Marquis d'Aubigné.............Mr. William T. Car

The opera is full of attractive musical fe ures, and, aside from the lovely waltz s which makes the theme of the work, in a

MARQUIS DE MARSILLAC IN "NANON.

the three acts there are many numbers a ing admirably melodious and well develop ideas. There is a character in all of Gené compositions which shows his individual as a writer, and his music is of the sort wh gains favor with repeated hearings. Amo the notable successes of last evenin performance are to be named interpolated song, sung by the Marquis d'A bigné in the first act, "Open thy lattice" (peated); the famous waltz song (repeated every introduction of the melody), the ch acter song and dance of Nanon's relativ upon assembling for her wedding, the fin of the first act; the song of the Marquis Marsillac, "I am an impressario" (repeate the duet for Nanon and the Marq d'Aubigné, the topical song by Hector, "I only a question of time," and the finale of t second act (repeated). Like most con operas, the best numbers, it will be observ are found in the first two acts, but the repe tion of the waltz song in the last act leaves pleasant impression of the work, and its mu cal characteristics appear to be well suit to give it as great popularity here it has already enjoyed in other cities. Th performance of the opera was, as a who characterized by an amount of spirit a dash which went far to make amends for t lack of finish in the presentation of son of the leading numbers and the ge eral effect of the work, as given this occasion, was highly enjoyab The heavy responsibility put upon t Marquis d'Aubigné was admirably sustai

SALON OF NINON DE L'ENCLOS IN "NANON."

MARQUIS D'AUBIGNE IN "NANON."

carried through the more dignified scenes [th]e last two acts with equal success. His [voic]e was in much better form than when [hear]d here last, and his singing was as ar[tisti]c and enjoyable as ever. The title rôle [was] given a capital impersonation by Miss [...]lin, who has developed in every way

carefully drawn picture of the favorite hostess of the Golden Lamb, and she maintained the character with equal success throughout the opera. Her voice, though not of remarkable sweetness, is true and of pleasant quality, and is used with intelligence and skill. Miss Alice Vincent adds a striking figure to the cast as Ninon de l'Enclos, and the limited vocal and dramatic demands of the rôle were fairly well filled. Miss Clara Wisdom made a fine appearance as Mme. de Maintenon, "the uncrowned Queen of France," and presented a picture of rare beauty as she sat at her table during the opening scene of the last act. Mr. Charles H. Drew, as Marquis de Marsillac, contributed the comedy element of the several scenes, and gained general favor by his spirited action, his singing of the song "I am an impresario," with the accompanying dance, making one of the evening's hits. Mr. Lehmann was equally successful as the bashful nephew, and created quite a sensation by his topical song, "It's only a question of time," though some changes in the verses might be made with advantage. Mr. Greensfelder has not been heard here for several seasons, and has profited much during his absence. His singing of the waltz song as a hymn, in the last act, gained an encore, and its interpretation was worthy of this recognition. The distribution of the minor characters was well made, and the chorus is an admirably chosen body of singers. The orchestra at times almost overpowered the singers, and there was at all times a sad lack of light and shade in the presentation of the orchestral score. It is unfortunate that the costumes of the company were not more generally renewed, as the bright scenes provided for the several acts made the imperfections in this department [mo]re prominent. The opera is announced as the attraction here until further notice.

"NANON."

Monday's Grand Production at the Hollis Street.

Zell and Genee's Famous Work to be Sung by the Carleton Opera Company.

Brilliant Costumes and Elegant Sce-

Everybody **has** heard about "Nanon." Did it not run **for** months in Vienna an[d] Berlin, and **at the** New York Casino, di[d] not the opera prove a veritable **lyric** lode star for 200 performances?

Zell wrote the book in the original Ger man, and Sydney Rosenfeld "overset" it, to speak Teutonically, into a language un derstanded of the people in America. Th[e] score is by Richard Genee, who has give[n] the world so many melodious measures.

"Anna, zu Dir ist mein liebster Gang" i[s] the gem of the opera. This delightfu[l] waltz song has been introduced often in th[e] course of "Nanon," and always to charmin[g] effect. This morceau has been interpolate[d] in many of the light opera performances o[f] the time. But in "Nanon" it is of cours[e] heard to especial advantage.

What is the **opera** all about? It take[s] the public back **to the** reign of Louis XIV to Paris in the days of Ninon de l'Enclo[s] and Mme. de Maintenon.

Three scenes suffice to present the stor[y]. The opening act is at the inn of the Golde[n] Lamb, near the gates of Paris. Then th[e] locale changes to the brilliant salon o[f] Ninon, the perennially beautiful; and th[e] last act passes in the sanctuary of the roya[l] favorite, De Maintenon.

Nanon herself, though renowned for vi[r]tue as well as beauty, occupies no highe[r] station than the hostess of this self-sam[e] Golden Lamb. Yet the king himself ha[s] seen and admired her; and the handsom[e] Marquis d'Aubigne, beloved by De l'Enclo[s] has been made a willing slave to he[r] charms. Under the disguise of a drumme[r] who is known as Grignan, the marquis woo[s] Nanon, and lays an elaborate scheme t[o] carry away the attractive maiden.

How these ingenious plans fail; how th[e] disguised nobleman, arrested on charge o[f] duelling and in danger of death, enlists i[n] his cause not only Nanon, but Ninon, ma[y] well be left for the opera itself to tell.

There's a coil, indeed, when the marqui[s] lover of Nanon, another marquis and a[n] amorous-minded abbe meet in the salon o[f] De l'Enclos. There is a duel before mat ters are cleared up, even for the time be ing and the consequences of that contest i[n] Ninon's garden are seen throughout th[e] third act of the opera. In the very sanctu ary of the favorite of the king, Nanon, th[e] inn-keeper, and Ninon, the leader of fash ion, humbly sue for [merc]y fo[r] their respective lovers, d'Aubigne an[d] Grignan. Nanon receives the lif[e] of Grignan as a present from the king, an[d] she in turn presents the pardon to Nanon h[...]

[illegible] happy [illegible]

[illegible] Production Will Be Most Elegant.

[illegible] the opera is certain to have every ad- [illegible] that managerial outlay can secure, [illegible] in giving "Nanon" an ornate stage [illegible] equalled on the American stage, [illegible] value of the opera will by no [illegible] unconsidered.

[illegible] Carleton opera company, it is gen- [illegible] Genée's music to better [illegible] the artists who appeared at the [illegible] York Casino.

[illegible] William T. Carleton, who appears as [illegible] needs no introduction to a [illegible] audience. His handsome presence [illegible] bearing will fit the role, and his fine [illegible] is said to be never smoother or [illegible] effective than now.

[illegible] Paulin, who was the origi- [illegible] in "Fantine," and who made [illegible] popular in "Zenita," is to be the Na- [illegible] and a very attractive hostess of the [illegible] Lamb she will doubtless prove to [illegible]

[illegible] Vincent is to be the Ninon, and Clara [illegible] the Maintenon. An old favorite of [illegible] days—none other than the original [illegible] in "Olivette" in this country— [illegible] in the Abbe. Joseph S. Greens- [illegible] is announced to be a better singer [illegible] than ever.

[illegible] H. Drew will be the Marquis de [illegible] and C. M. Lenmane the nephew, [illegible] he seeks to introduce to [illegible] the French capital.

[illegible] general cast is long, and it intro- [illegible] favorites. There will be a very [illegible] and as the company has [illegible] successfully in many cities, [illegible] ensemble performance is to [illegible] anticipated.

[illegible] will be evoked by the scenery [illegible] It is the work of that skilful [illegible] John A. Thompson, regularly [illegible] with the Hollis Street. Already [illegible] his work for "Nanon" but [illegible]

[illegible] in the opening scene, with [illegible] poplars that stand out from the [illegible] lookout upon a real [illegible] scene, and not a picture, is really [illegible] The Seine is visible in the back- [illegible] with the city in the distance, while [illegible] left the little inn is to be seen; and [illegible] setting is admirable in its [illegible] of perspective effects, and in [illegible] of the exterior of the Golden [illegible]

[illegible] elegant interiors are shown in the [illegible] The salon of Ninon de l'Enclos, [illegible] of the conservatory to the [illegible] the grand staircase which opens [illegible] is a very brilliant piece of color- [illegible] Very elaborate, too, is the setting [illegible] the sanctuary of Maintenon, [illegible] architectural effects and furnishings [illegible] scene, illuminated through stained [illegible] windows at the rear, will repay close [illegible]

[illegible]ANON'S" PRETTY COSTUMES.

[illegible] of the Beauties of the Wardrobe of Carleton's Company.

[illegible] the promises made on behalf of "Na- [illegible]" shall be realized the ladies will find [illegible] much more in the opera comique of [illegible] to them besides melodious music [illegible] handsome men and women. Fine [illegible] is made one of the chief [illegible] of "Nanon," and as several [illegible] the costumes possess the charm of [illegible] a description of one or two will [illegible] to indicate the general character of [illegible] work the dressmakers have been doing [illegible] the production.

[illegible] as D'Aubigne, will appear in a [illegible] white satin, with diamonds under his [illegible] and in his buttons and buckles, while [illegible] his breast is gathered enough fleecy [illegible] to enrich a Commonwealth avenue [illegible] for life. A delicate thread of gold [illegible] is broidered in the satin, and the [illegible] of the entire costume will doubtless [illegible] very beautiful.

[illegible] beauty of Nanon's clothes lies more [illegible] harmony of their colors than in the [illegible] for Nanon is but the hostess of a [illegible] little inn outside the gates of Paris. [illegible] will wear a pale blue skirt with [illegible] drapery and wine-colored bodice. [illegible]'s toilette in the second act will be [illegible] enough, they say, to put an [illegible] on feu de respiration the moment [illegible] Vincent enters upon the stage. The [illegible] of white satin embellished with [illegible] lilies, nasturtiums, pinks and fern [illegible] stamped in the goods. The same [illegible] texture constitutes the bodice, but [illegible] up the front and down again [illegible] left hip like lines of grace are two [illegible] of [illegible] lace in colored silks. [illegible] forty-four inches of white ribbon [illegible] the right shoulder, but an ostrich- [illegible] at the end [illegible] in the hair and about the square [illegible]

NINON DE L'ENCLOS IN "NANON."

about a graceful throat, jewel the ears, pin a small star above the forehead in the pompadour of yellow hair and, says one who has seen "Nanon," you have one of the loveliest toilets that ever moved a woman to envy.

In the same act will be two other hand-some toilets, one being a dreamy sort of a heliotrope brocade with embossed satin petticoat and pale pink plumes for the head and corsage.

Charles H. Drew, as Marsillac, will appear in long Louis XIV. trunks of cranberry satin, with silk hose and shoes to match, and a coat and waistcoat of embroidered white satin.

C. M. Lenmane, as Hector, will wear a lovely costume of pale pink satin in this same act, and in the former one a brocaded velvet coat with light blue satin trunks.

Miss Clara Wisdom, as Mme. de Maintenon, will appear in the third act in a long princesse of black lustreless silk made with jetted front, with a ruche of white lace at the bottom. The neck is cut perfectly square, the sleeves halting just above the dimpled elbow. In her hair is worn a star of jet.

Mr. Carleton will also wear in this last act a beautiful black satin costume heavily beaded and decorated.

Besides these, there are some decided novelties, such as the costumes worn by the drummers of the Royal Guards and others worn by the pretty band of violinists, but no one would dare to attempt to describe them—or at least what there is of them—and they must be seen to be appreciated.

MUSIC AND THE DRAMA.

"NANON" AT THE HOLLIS STREET THEATRE.

The Hollis Street Theatre changed its programme for the first time last night, and entertained a large and brilliant audience with the initial performance of "Nanon" in Boston. "Nanon" is a three act comic opera, the music of which was composed by Genée and the text by F. Zell, the libretto having been put into English by Mr. Sydney Rosenfeld. The piece has had long runs in several of the European capitals, and at the New York Casino it was performed for many months. There is little doubt that it will be successful here. It has, aside from its intrinsic merits, the charm of an elegant setting and the splendor reflected from numerous and well trained auxiliaries brilliantly attired.

The story of the opera is simple enough. The period is that of Louis XIV., and *Ninon de l'Enclos* and *Mme. de Maintenon*, as well as the great monarch himself, appear among the dramatis personae. The heroine, *Nanon Patin*, hostess of the Golden Lamb, a hearty, prosperous country lassie, vivacious but chaste, is wooed by the elegant *Marquis d'Aubigne*, who, in the disguise of a humble drummer—not the commercial sort—has won her hitherto unconquered heart. She supposes his intentions to be honorable, and just after the opera begins has arranged as a delightful surprise for him their solemn union before the notary in the presence of all her humble kinsfolk. This attention proves exceedingly embarrassing to the noble *Marquis*, who saves himself at the critical moment when his signature is demanded to the marriage contract, by an arrest of himself, which he has planned, the pretext of which is [illegible] s of the weeping *Nanon* he is thus ; and in the second act she follows to Paris in order to secure the rvention in behalf of her drummer lover of on *de l'Enclos*, who has seen her and pro- n her assistance. The second act is at on's house, where *D'Aubigne* is presently severed paying court to the reigning beauty foretime. The fun and few complications he piece come from *Nanon's* turning up in salon of *Ninon*, meeting her lover , but not fairly recognizing him his elegant dress, and finally at e *de Maintenon's* house, securing by an odd take the favor of the *King* himself and a par- for her lover, who by this time has actually ngered his safety by taking part in a real l. Before the end is reached *Nanon* has ed out her lover's true name and doubtful ty, but *D'Aubigne*, like a true lover, accepts late and situation, and, renouncing his ced gallantries, promises before the cur- falls to marry her. Two noble- , an uncle and nephew, who ed *Nanon* at her inn and there made the ac- ntance of her drummer lover and were itted by him help to make the stuff of the thick and slab in ways which it boots not to idder; and *D'Aubigne's* pretty song, originally posed in *Nanon's* honor, becomes the source ench fun, as it is used by the *Marquis* in r of *De l'Enclos* and is stolen by his friends the repertoire of the supposed drummer.

e libretto is much more ingenious than the l translated libretto, and as a literary work credit to Mr. Rosenfeld's taste and skill in oth writing and neat rhyming. But what- wit Mr. Zell put into his text—if he per- ed any such feat—has utterly evaporated in process of transportation and transplantation the vernacular. It is therefore a different kind of fun which the ligent auditor will expect to find here from which he is sure to meet in Mr. Gilbert's irable texts. The libretto has in itself st no power to entertain and the amusement rived, if derived at all, from that part of the er's wit or humor which has survived in ations in stage "business" and in the tion of characters which may be made ring by amusing performers. There is a erate amount of this kind of humble fun to be d in portions of "Nanon," but, of course, e is no sustained drollery in the piece, and e are long reaches of commonplace, slashed interspersed with foolishness. The names ome of the female characters may seem er alarming, but decency has been scrupu- ly preserved and none of the scenes is at all ssive. The best bit of humor in the piece,— the most characteristic,—is found in the age where the innocent *Nanon* addresses the y as "Monsieur Maintenon," supposing him the original of his "wife's" portrait of him.

e music is a different matter, and though not ked by genius or by the imprint of even the est forms of talent, it is so bright, so odious and in its best moments so sweet and inating as to insure a great deal of delight very lover of pleasant tunes. The often re- al lover's air—

What is this day
That seems to say
Life is most wondrous fair?

already become very familiar. It certainly much charm, and it is varied by no little in- uity as it is devoted by turns to the praise of on, of *Ninon* and of *De Maintenon*, and is ously rehearsed by *D'Aubigne, De Marsillac* the *Abbe*. Many of the concerted numbers interesting, all the finales being spirited and viously complicated and that of the second essentially humorous. The duet between on and her lover in the second act is dis- uished by a finer fitting of sound to sense is usual in the opera.

e performance, of varying degrees of merit s separate parts and portions, is as a whole be commended. The ensemble effects are llent. The chorus is large, and shows good ; the orchestra is kept well in hand, and in concerted music the careful preparation of opera by Mr. Carleton and his assistants is y apparent. Smoothness, brilliancy and spirit the prevailing traits in all this portion of the formance. When separate performers are sidered, it is found that Mr. Carleton is the y really fine singer, and that of the other prin- ls, Miss Paulin and Mr. Lenmane are the y ones with voices fairly equal to the de- nds of the occasion, neither of these being liant, and the former displaying much hard-ness of quality. Mr. Carleton takes the part of the hero, looks it as if he had drunk of Ponce de Leon's fount, and acts with sufficient grace, spirit and taste to meet the exacting require- ments of the character very well indeed. His voice and style of singing are, of course, very well known; and it is but moderate praise to say that they are far above the voice and style to which we have all been inured in this kind of opera. Miss Paulin ap- pears as *Nanon*, and sings her music correctly and vigorously, in the hard fashion already described. As an actress she is unequal, but, on the whole, achieves decided success. Of serious and pathetic effects she has, apparently, the dim- mest notion; but in humor she is strong, and her delivery of the reiterated lines, "Oh! isn't he sweet?" is so shrewd and sharply direct as to be almost memorable, while her action and pantomime of self disgust and surprise when she learns *De l'Enclos's* real name in the first act approach the masterly. Miss Alice Vincent is a very handsome *Ninon*, and her acting is toler- able, but her voice is harsh and needs to be modulated with great cleverness that it may not be positively disagreeable. Miss Josephine Bart- lett is acceptable as the page, *Gaston*, and Miss Clara Wisdom deserves a fair word for her *Mme. de Maintenon*. The leading male characters in the support are taken by Mr. Charles H. Drew, Mr. Lenmane and Mr. Greensfelder, who appear respectively as the *Marquis de Marsillac, Hector Vicomte de Mar- sillac* and the *Abbe*. Mr. Drew has a rough and rancorous voice, and has lost most of his ability to please as a singer. As an actor he shows a good deal of resource and rapidity as well as native comic power and the skill born of experience; unfortunately he does not know when or where to stop, and he frequently allows his humor to degenerate into buffoonery or mere silliness. Mr. Lenmane sings smoothly, and in action shows a neat, mild, but not unacceptable type of easy comicality. Upon him is put the dangerous honor of deliver- ing the interpolated stanzas—which with their political and "local" allusions are now inevitable in every operetta—and this feat he achieves with modesty, the verses themselves, though common- place, being, for a wonder, smooth, decent, and not devoid of sense. As the *Abbe* Mr. Greens- felder shows that his ideas of humorous action are rudimentary, but his singing is quite good.

It has been said that the setting of the piece is excellent. Special mention should be made of the elegance of the scenic sets, all of which are well painted. The contrasts between the rustic life of the first act, the elaborate splendor of *De l'Enclos's* house in the second act, and the severe simplicity of *De Maintenon's* oratory in the third act, are made very effective not only through the canvas but by propriety of costume and appointments. The audience seemed greatly pleased and applause and repetitions abounded.

A CHORUS GIRL IN "NANON."

DRAMATIC AND MUSICAL.

"Nanon."

The Hollis Street Theatre last night was filled with an interested audience of first nighters, who had come to see the inauguration of a new comic opera in this theatre, where the "Mikado" has so long held sway. "Nanon" was the attraction, and it had as presages of success the reports of long runs in other cities at home and abroad. It has been somewhat a matter of surprise that a work which was said to have won so high favor elsewhere has not before this been heard in Bos- ton. But that much interest had been awakened in the new production was evidenced by the char- acter, as well as the size, of last night's audience. Gov. Robinson and staff, Mayor O'Brien, President Pillsbury of the Mas- sachusetts Senate and Speaker Brackett of the House occupied boxes, while a num- ber of prominent city officials and mem- bers of society were in the orchestra seats. The leading motive of "Nanon" is the serenade, "Anna, in Rapture I Come to Thee," a song which is heard now here and now there, now sung by one character and now by another, and now to one fair lady and now to a second and a third, for the dramatic complication of the piece makes each of the three leading ladies have the pet name of Anna and leaves each plagiarizing singer in bliss- ful ignorance that what he claims to be original is really known to the hearer as an "old story." Mr. William T. Carleton, as the Marquis d'Aubigne disguised as the drummer Grignan, first sings the lay to Nanon, who, as hostess of the Golden Lamb, a modest little inn just outside the gates of Paris, has fallen in love with the handsome young soldier. But d'Aubigne is in no hurry for a mar- riage, and so, when wedding guests make their appearance, at the invitation of the heroine, he causes himself to be arrested by his Colonel on the charge of dueling. Nanon (Miss Louise P. Paulin), in grief, goes to the salon of Ninon de l'Enclos, a famous beauty, to seek her aid in se- curing a pardon, as dueling is punishable by death. As it happens, d'Aubigne, under his true name, is a follower of Ninon (Miss Alice Vincent), and to her he sings his double-faced serenade, "Anna, in Rapture I Come to Thee." Then Mr. Charles H. Drew, as the Marquis de Mar- sillac, takes his turn, after d'Aubigne's departure, at the much-used favorite song. Having noticed its effect when Grignan sang it to Nanon he at- tempts the same effect upon Ninon, but only gets laughed at for his pains. Meanwhile d'Aubigne and Hector, a young country nobleman (Mr. C. N. Lenmane), being both rivals for the affections of Nanon and Ninon, have had a duel, and Hector is wounded. In the third act the motive of the serenade is again heard, for now the third Anna, Mme. de Maintenon (Miss Clara Wisdom), has to listen to the good Abbe (Mr. Joseph S. Greensfelder), as he chants the serenade in the form of a pious hymn. Now d'Aubigne is a nephew of Mme. de Maintenon, and, accordingly, unaware that his ballad has been so often pirated, he pays his respects to his aunt on her birthday with the same serenade. This complicates still further the credit for the origin of the song. Finally Nanon secures Grignan's pardon, and having found out that the drummer is really d'Aubigne, she gives the pardon to Ninon that she may save their mutual lover. This nobleness wins the heart of the drum- mer-marquis, and he offers himself in good earnestness to the hostess of the little inn.

"Nanon" in its entirety pleases by its continuance of easy-running, melodious music, rather than by any especial brilliancy in any song. The music is graceful and bright, and while it does not have the ... weight of some other opera music of the same class, it yet fulfils the function of the time by giving enjoyment for the time being. There is a strong tendency toward the waltz movement, a movement which is always popular and which pro- duces the greatest charm in music, to enable it to carry the listener along fully in sympathy with scenes of pleasure. The leading song, "Anna, in Rapture, I Come to Thee," is a waltz of this char- acter, pretty and charming, and one most likely of all the airs to be remembered. A second song which won particular notice was Hector's selection, "It's all a question of time." Its popularity was gained more by the words than by the music, it being one of the so-called "topical songs" and really treating of present affairs in a higher vein and with less nonsense than the average song of that character. The allusion in one verse to the "Democrat" and the "Republican" was ... by Hector's pointing to the box of the Governor as that of the "Democrat" and to the box of the Mayor as that of the "Republican." Finally, when encores had closed the list of verses, he sang with appropriate effect, "I must stop soon, or I'll drop soon; it's only a question of time," and the audience took the hint. The opera is very well rendered by the Carleton Company. The voices are good and the acting is spirited, with the liveliness of word and briskness of motion necessary to hold attention closely. As the opera has a great abundance of music, with little of the spoken text, there is a special neces- sity also for good singing in all the parts. The chorus are, perhaps, overheavy for the Hollis Street stage, but that is a commendable fault in comparison with weakness or timidity of ensemble singing. In the first act the song and dance of the double quartette is especially well done, while the ... is given by each of the neighbors of Nanon, who have come to congratulate her on her wedding day, bearing some live animal, hen, pig or goose, or a big Dutch cheese. This was the first song to start the hearty laughter of the audience that

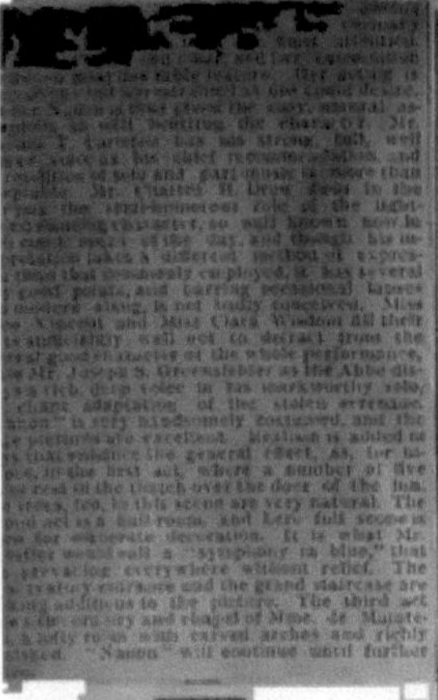

... and fair representation ... Her acting is ... Nanon, as sung, ... her ... Mr. Charles H. Drew ... Miss Clara Wisdom ... Mr. Joseph S. Greensfelder as the Abbe ... "Nanon" is very handsomely costumed, and the ... It is what Mr. ... would call a "symphony in blue," that prevailing everywhere without relief. The ... entrance and the grand staircase are ... additions to the picture. The third act ... and chapel of Mme. de Mainte... lofty room with carved arches and richly ... "Nanon" will continue until further ...

...onday night, for the second time only since the new ...atre was opened, the Hollis-street held a first-...ht audience. To succeed the "Mikado" a popular ...ess in the line of French operatic adaptation, ...ee's "Nanon" had been chosen; a work as differ-... in spirit as could be imagined. It was presented ...the Carleton Opera Company for the first time ...Boston with the following cast:

...non Patis, Hostess of the Golden Lamb.............Miss Louise E. Paullin
...on de L'Enclos.............Miss Alice Vincent
...e. de Maintenon.............Miss Clara Wisdom
...quis de Marsillac.............Mr. Charles H. Drew
...tor Vicompte de Marsillac, nephew of Marquis
...e Marsillac.............Mr. C. M. Lewname
...e.............Mr. Joseph S. Greensfelder
...g Louis XIV.............Mr. Tom Guise
...rquis D'Aubigne.............Mr. William T. Carleton

...he music is by Genee, the libretto by F. Zell, ...nslated into American by Mr. Sydney Rosenfeld. ...e Carleton Company has given the opera at ... New York Casino, and in different parts of ... country. The book of the play has a begin-...g, an ending and considerable narrative matter ...way, differing in this respect from some of the ...ream types of comic opera which have lately been ...en here. A condensed version of it would read ...ething like this: Nanon, the hostess of the ...olden Lamb," both beautiful and moral, has had ... heart touched by the feigned suit of Grignan, a ...mmer, (one who beats a drum,) who as the Marquis ...Aubigne, in disguise, seeks only to amuse himself ...h her. On the occasion of a serenade to Nanon, ...ich Grignan and his pretended associates arrange, ...evening before her birthday, Nanon proposes to ...ignan that they be married. To extricate himself ...Aubigne, when the wedding guests, the notary and ...non's relatives are assembled, causes his own ar-...t for duelling, a crime punishable by death, and ...rried away. Consonant with the features thus ...disclosed, is the the appearance on the scene the ... before the wedding was so rudely inter-...ted, of Ninon de L'Enclos, who is suspicious that ... lover (D'Aubigne) is paying court to Nanon. ...ving arrived at the Golden Lamb to hear only that ...non is to marry a drummer, she departs consoled ... to D'Aubigne's absence. Now, Nanon, ... her misery at the arrest of Grignan, ...ks Ninon's aid who has influence ...th ...e. de Maintenon, the king's favorite, to ...tore to her her lover. Act first brings the story ...this point, having also introduced the helpful ...racter of DeMarsillac and Hector, his nephew, as ...sodes upon the dramatic camera. The second ... changes to the salon of Ninon. Nanon has fol-...wed her to Paris to forward Grignan's release. ...re she encounters D'Aubigne, but his disguise ...ceals his identity. Again, in the third act, Nanon ...successful, through a lucky error which brings ...r into the presence of the king at Mme. de Mainte-...n's, in securing a pardon for Grignan. After the ...nner of tales of this kind, Nanon has penetrated ...e disguise of D'Aubigne, who, having himself en-...ged in a real duel on Ninon's account, is likewise ...e object of a plea from her for his pardon. Nanon ...nsfers the king's pardon of Grignan (now a vis-...nary character) to Ninon, that D'Aubigne may be ...ed. This touches the heart of the gay reveller, ...d he meets Nanon's sacrifice by marrying her. It and continuing of the piece. The leit-motif of the work (to use a grandiloquent phrase), is the melody, "Nanon I come to thee," which is used successively by Grignan, Marsillac and the Abbe, with the most amusing disregard of copyright obligations. The lines of Nanon are not irreproachable in point of sweet ness. Hector introduces a song, "It's only a question of time," where the avoidance of distasteful suggestiveness is not successfully accomplished, and the innocent Nanon, though a guileless person, has on occasions a rather fluent vocabulary. Mr. Rosenfeld did not find in M. Zell a highly intellectual incentive, but he has performed legitimate work, and if there is little that is fanciful or elegant in his translation, the avoirdupois of the piece is sufficiently French to float it; and its liveliness of movement, especially in the first act, its contrasting situations affording opportunities for brilliant stage settings which were handsomely undertaken in the presentation of last night, and the happy buoyancy and bright sparkle of the music will doubtless make it as attractive to Boston audiences as it has proven in other places. The situations, while always chosen with tact and skill and combining many unique features, such as the chorus and procession of Nanon's relatives at the wedding festivities in the first act, seldom show a real dramatic grip; an anti-climax is often reached. But, to take the third act as an illustration, while it presents some humorous situations, it closes negatively. There is neither a strong musical movement nor does the denouement of the piece occur at the point where the curtain falls. The audience should depart with a bit of a tune or the impression retained from some final situation. To specify in detail the many pleasant and tuneful numbers in the musical score seems unnecessary. As has been intimated, there is a gracious turn throughout all the music; dance rhythms abound; a pretty melody is often daintily set in the orchestra, and the choruses are effective. The melody of "Nanon, I come to thee," makes a very singable number. The performance had a lively swing and ease which bespoke sureness on the part of all the principals. Mr. Carleton naturally claims first attention. The part of the Marquis is an agreeable one for him; a good figure and manifest physical gifts, a fine voice and easy stage ways make his impersonation acceptable, while his singing is unusually good, as need not be said at this late day, when rated with others in this line of work. Yet as a vocalist he has decided faults of voice production; a faulty habit of enunciation which loses quickly the vowel form where its continuance would not only insure a better tone, but give his voice a greater carrying power. His song to Nanon was repeated as were nearly all the vocal numbers which fell to him singly or in concert. Miss Paullin as Nanon gave a pretty and consistent sketch. She sings with animation, her enunciation of the spoken text is clear, and she has an habitual stage manner which is always a reliance, while it shows her the possessor of considerable versatility. Miss Vincent has abundant natural charms, and looked well the careless Ninon of the demi-monde, while she dressed the part elegantly. Her vocal gifts are not commensurate with those of nature, and she is to be commended for not showing in her singing that she thought they were. Mr. Drew as the volatile Marsillac, who, not yet himself aloof from being a gallant, has the perilous task of initiating a nephew (Hector) into the conventionalities of that questionable existence which knows no consequences, supplied a comedy element which was creditable in that it abstained from being unduly broad, while it had some unctuous touches. Mr. Lewname acted the part of Hector with that lassitude of demeanor which many a real simpleton could not have improved. He is the central figure of a funny scene which ends the second act, and carried neatly his part in the musical ensemble which accompanies it, though he hasn't a particularly musical voice, nor is it likely that he intends publishing a treatise on the "art of singing." His is the only tenor part in the work. Mr. Greensfelder, as the amorous Abbe, was a darksome picture, both in garb and as to the intent of the part in burlesquing an order of the clergy. We see no chance of condoning such a creation. His turn with the melody of the Serenade to Nanon came in the last act, where he made considerable impression by his parody in a deep bass voice. The part of Mme. de Maintenon by Miss Wisdom is only an etching in black and white, while that of the King by Mr. Guise is short and sweet. Praise can be given the two ladies who served as attendants to Ninon. The courtly grace of she whose robe was of pink made her an attractive picture throughout the performance. The orchestra is not quiet enough; its work is fairly acceptable, but in the accompaniments often overpowers the voices, the cornet player needing some urgent subduing. As was expected the stage setting of the work, particularly the scenes in Ninon's salon and at Mme. de Maintenon's, was artistically of great elegant material. We should add that the chorus is very good, the group of drummers and fifers and what miniature pageantry there was being noticeably in excellent hands. An audience which filled the theatre attested its pleasure in the performance by repeated encores. The opera will continue for the present at the theatre with the usual matinee performances.

"NANON" AT THE HOLLIS STREET THEATRE. —It was a large and merry audience that assembled in the Hollis Street Theatre on Monday evening, and many were there no doubt who had come prepared to find Richard Genée's "Nanon" quite as enchanting a vehicle of mirth and joyousness as had for so many months enhanced the fame of "The Mikado." It required but a brief experience with the opening scenes of the new opera in order to discover that the work in progress bordered very closely upon the domain of legitimate comic opera, and that no such sequence of fun-creating incidents could be expected as had made the light and frivolous yet ever bewitching Mikado the bouffe par excellence of the season. Another such success indeed is not to be desired. It has come to this, namely: that comic opera must necessarily be allied to a mediocre form of art; it must be over-crowded with short and evanescent pieces, in which shall inhere a downright cheapness of musical merit, that never rises above the level of a quasi-prettiness. Such is the comic opera of the period, and such, to an extent that is not wholly unpraiseworthy, is "Nanon." Its pretty ballads, lively choruses and spirited dance music, and especially its book, and the dialogue therein, are adequately characteristic of a decline that has taken place in comic opera during the past century. It is a decline that the theatre-going public has fostered and encouraged to an almost unlimited extent.

To admit all this without being over-fastidious in regard to the standpoint of observation, and also to acknowledge the general praiseworthiness in almost constant attendance upon the present performance of the work, virtually admits that "Nanon" has entered upon a brief season of well-merited prosperity at the new Hollis Street Theatre. As usual, the composer of the music has the best of it. Otherwise the work merits success on account of the time-serving decency of its musical development. The harmlessly low order of the "book," so called, is yet untainted by anything that even a prude would regard as either vulgar, coarse, unseemly or immoral. There is little in attendance calculated to rouse the merriment of the hearer to a high pitch of hilarity, but it is a respectable book. It is not without plot, but we all know that plots have long since ceased to form an indispensable element in the success of any kind of opera. Nanon is represented as a very attractive young girl, who lived in the time of Louis Fourteenth. Despite the nearness of her age to that of youth, she was the hostess of an inn called "The Golden Lamb." The nobility were in the habit of visiting this inn, and the pretty Nanon no doubt often participated in a harmless flirtation with lords of high degree, yet she retained her beauty, and was noted far and wide for her virtue. The Marquis d'Aubigne became enamored of Nanon. Loving her, he would not only woo but wed her. It was the same old story. She, a p. v. peasant girl; and he a naughty Marquis. Mistaking his attentions as those of a sincere and honest suitor, Nanon arranges for their marriage, in order to evade which the Marquis has himself arrested by the colonel of his own regiment. The arrest takes place just as the gay deceiver is called upon by the notary to sign the marriage contract, in the presence of the most grotesque and paysanne appearing set of sisters and cousins and aunts that were ever made the subject of histrionism. The notary lost his commission that time. In the meanwhile, Ninon de l'Enclos has been informed of the flirtation of the Marquis. Ninon—not Nanon—has many admirers in the court of Louis XIV., but her favorite is the Marquis. Ninon had sought out her rival, the peasant girl, who innocently dispels her jealousy by informing her that she, namely, Nanon, is about to marry a drummer named Grignan. This Grignan must have been a very bad drummer, for he is the Marquis in disguise. Nanon appeals to Ninon to use her influence for the pardon of the Marquis, who is imprisoned for having engaged in a duel. The remainder of the plot, stripped of its incidents, may be easily guessed.

A unique character in the cast is that of Hector Vicompte de Marsillac, nephew of Marquis de Marsillac. The uncle is depicted as a man of tact, a skilful swordsman, something of a comedian...

D'Aubigne likewise appears, [illegible] of Ninon, and when she reproaches him for having stayed away so long and for having forgotten her birthday, he sings to her the same serenade that he had previously sung in the first act to Nanon. Soon Nanon arrives, but does not recognize D'Aubigne as Grignan. Marsillac, who has heard Grignan's serenade, also offers that as his tribute to Ninon, and is laughed at as having stolen the song. Hector and D'Aubigne fight a duel on account of the former's attentions to Ninon, and Hector is wounded in the hip and is arrested, refusing to give the name of his opponent.

The Third Scene

is laid in the audience chamber of Mme. de Maintenon, whose name is Anna also, and the abbe sings to her in the shape of a pious hymn, and with hypocritical intent, the serenade. Marsillac secures his nephew's delivery, as a chance betrayed that D'Aubigne, who is a nephew of Mme. de Maintenon, gave the challenge. D'Aubigne congratulates her on her birthday with the same serenade, and Marsillac after him, so that the war over the origin of the song rises anew. Nanon receives the life of Grignan as a present from the King, and she presents the pardon to Ninon in order to save d'Aubigne, in whom she now recognizes Grignan. Touched by so much magnanimity, Grignan offers his hand to her; the Maintenon, displeased by the sudden favor of the King for Nanon, gives her consent, and the hostess of the "Golden Lamb" is made Marquise d'Aubigne.

The thoroughly interesting character of the opera can, perhaps, scarcely be derived from this hasty sketch of the plot. It will be noted that the work is really based upon the waltz song, "Anna, in Rapture I Come to Thee," which is made to do duty again and again as a serenade. Much of the movement of plot and much of the musical beauty of the opera comes from this single number, and its appropriation and misappropriation by all the characters as occasion offers. This is a very happy conceit of the composer and librettist, and as the number is of itself very charming, the effect is in the highest degree satisfying. There are other charming numbers in the work, and the score as a whole is exceedingly brilliant, inspiring and musicianly.

The performance last evening was admirable. Principals and support alike entered into their work with spirit, and gave the work an exceedingly brilliant and artistic interpretation.

The principal success of the evening was achieved by

Mr. William T. Carleton,

as the Marquis d'Aubigne. He dressed and acted the part superbly, and sang with good judgment and excellent expression throughout. He has a full, strong voice, that is sweet and resonant, and he uses it in a splendid manner. His singing of the serenade was encored as often as it was given.

Miss Louise Paullin

was a charming Nanon. She looked the part beautifully and acted gracefully and with charming piquancy and naivete. She sang the music allotted to the character in a fresh, unaffected manner and invested it with an enticing charm of expression.

The Ninon of Miss Alice Vincent and the Mme. de Maintenon of Miss Clara Wisdom was also admirably presented, and among the minor female parts those of Gaston by Miss Josephine Bartlett and the page of Miss Jessie Quigley merit special attention for gracefulness and ease of bearing.

Mr. Charles H. Drew invested the role of Marsillac with a great deal of opera bouffe character, and got a great deal of humor out of it. He showed here and there a tendency to gagging that is not to be commended. His singing was good, and his rendering of his bouffe number, "I Am an Impressario," was one of the hits of the evening. Mr. G. M. Lemmens as Hector was the inexperienced young man to perfection, and his number, "I'll Get There in Time," in the third act, was a strong feature in the performance. The other roles were acceptably filled. The chorus was strong in numbers and in volume of voice. Its members sang effectively and truly throughout.

The opera was magnificently staged. The three scenes are marvels of beauty, and the costuming is as elegant as anything seen on the local stage for a long time. In scenery, in costumes, in stage pictures, it is not often vouchsafed the theatregoer to see anything richer or more artistic. The scenery is the work of Mr. John A. Thompson, while the various effects have been arranged by Messrs. D. H. Craig, William O'Brien and Fred A. Cutler and their assistants, and the whole production is under the direction of Mr. William Dixon. The presentation is of such an exceptionally remarkable character as respects the work of these gentlemen that it is only just that particular credit should be accorded them.

The audience last evening was very large and brilliant, musical and social circles being largely represented. In the house were Governor Robinson and party, Mayor O'Brien and party, Speaker Brackett and party and President Pillsbury and party.

The Brilliant Great Mikado at the Globe Theatre.

A delightful libretto, bewitching music, elegant costumes and charming scenery gave to the large and critical audience at the Hollis Street Theatre last evening more enjoyment than enthusiastic predictions could have led any one to expect. "Nanon," the opera that had set Vienna and Berlin almost wild and has commanded the interest of New Yorkers for 200 successive performances, has established itself in Boston on a sound basis, which makes universal attraction and perfect satisfaction an assurance beyond doubt.

The audience was a most brilliant one, not only in point of numbers but in the large number of prominent officials and society people present. Governor Robinson and wife and Councillor Locke and lady oc-

NANON.

cupied the right proscenium box. His Honor Mayor O'Brien and wife and party of ladies filled Manager Rich's private box; the left balcony box was occupied by President Pillsbury of the Senate and State officials, and the right balcony box by Speaker Brackett of the House and ladies. Among many familiar faces in the audience was Julius Eichberg, Henry E. Raymond, Miss Raymond, Horace Chandler, Arthur Austin, Clark Hollingsworth, B. L. Arlocam, E. S. Hale, Jr., T. J. Homer, Colonel W. V. Hutchins, James Jordan, and others. Lord Parker, of London, was in the audience, an interested spectator. The toilets displayed by the ladies were exquisite, and it was the general verdict that a more brilliant audience has not been seen at this beautiful temple of the drama since the night of its opening.

When the curtain first arose, and before the audience stood in full light a brilliant autumn landscape scene just outside the walls of Paris, with the Seine flowing calmly in the background and on the left the entrance of the little inn, the Golden Lamb, it was evident from the general commotion that the house was more than pleased. Before the beauties of the scene could be fairly taken in the full, well-balanced music of a large chorus, in praise of the charms of Nanon, the lovely hostess, came forth from the picture with a zest that seemed to thrill every listener, and the

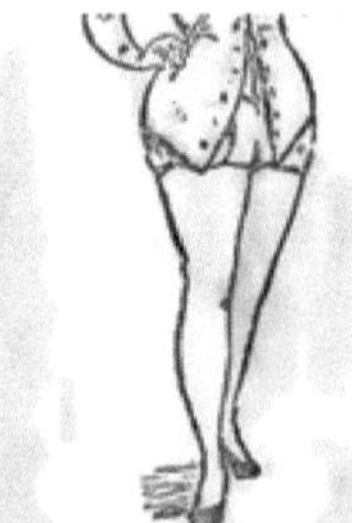

ONE OF TWENTY.

"For each thirsty guest" flowed "bright wine of the best" and the chorus grew more hearty and the chords richer. Nanon appeared in modest costume—pale blue skirt, with drapery and a wine-colored bodice. The part was impersonated by none other than

Pretty Louise Paullin,

whose magnetic voice and easy grace had already won for her distinction in "Fantine" and "Zanita," and a charming hostess she made. So rollicking was her manner and so accurate in attack and natural in expression was her voice, that the character which she portrayed seemed to be a part of her very nature. The audience fell into the best of humor and applause came plentifully, as a matter of necessity.

"ISN'T HE SWEET?"

Nanon off the scene, a manly form strode down the steps at the rear of the foreground of the scene, and "Oh! isn't he handsome?" was the exclamation that forced itself from the lips of more than one enthusiastic admiring lady. Yes, he was handsome. The theatregoers in New York had long before been free to assert the same opinion, and Will Carleton had made a hit in Boston before he had entered a [illegible]. Applause over and his prelude concluded, Nanon having again appeared, the Marquis d'Aubigne, disguised as a drummer [illegible] the double part which [illegible] the gem of the opera [illegible] in honor of St. Anne's day. This [illegible] the wonderful baritone of the artist [illegible] would begin to satisfy the [illegible]

in their original absurdity of color and cut. The nephew's sappy, "can't understand," goody-goody characteristic was brought out in a remarkably funny way by Mr. Lermans, his topical song, "It's Only a Question of Time," being the subject of encore after encore. The verses were of the very best, being pertinent and hitting facts of everyday experience, and were none of them in the least forced, but ran along, all of them, in a glib, tingling, taking way.

To the chorus no small quota of praise is due. In New York the chorus was one of the parts of the production which called out specially appreciative comment from critics, but it is certain that since the performances there this feature has been much improved, more fully rounded and pruned.

A FAIR DRUMMER.

The scenery was gorgeous in the extreme. The artist, John A. Thompson, has accomplished work which thoroughly merited the admiration which was showered upon it from all sides. The first scene seemed filled with real life. The trees stood out as in nature, the details of the exterior of the Golden Lamb were consistent and realistic, while the Seine appeared to be the peaceful river that it actually is, flowing slowly by the gay city in the distance. The other two scenes are interiors. The second represents the salon of Ninon de l'Enclos, giving a glimpse of a conservatory on the right, and at the rear centre a broad staircase opening gracefully at the left and another winding up on the right.

The Most Wonderful Point

in this brilliant scene is the perfect mastery of the problem of perspective, which, from every seat in the house, gives a correct view of the scenery in the rear, in no case distorted, in every particular pleasing to the eye. The sanctuary of Madame de Maintenon, shown in the last act, is, architecturally, a very impressive affair, and the effect of the furnishings and illumination through stained glass windows in the rear is remarkable, yet not overdone.

The costumes were worn for the first time last evening. They were much more expensive and elaborate than any which "Nanon" has had advantage of in this country. They have been described in detail in THE GLOBE, and so do not need further mention again.

"What made the performance so delightful?" was the question which naturally suggested itself when the excitement was over. "Was it the libretto, the music, the affecting pathos, and yet the offensive wit that so often creeps into works of this nature is wholly wanting in this instance, giving free enjoyment without trespassing at all upon a just sense of the decent. The music is characteristic of Genee, Frenchy, hence captivating—the one air which pervades the whole score especially so, and when looked at in the right light does not give the music as a whole any disagreeable sameness. Indeed it constitutes the peculiar charm of the composition.

The success of the opera is due to the aggregation and combination of so many beauties. That William Dixon, the stage manager, to whom this success is mostly due, has spared no pains to ensure a hit, is evident upon the least reflection. The stage mechanism, properties, calcium effects and costumes, under the direction of Messrs. D. B. Craig, William O'Brien, Fred A. Cutter and Mme. Loe respectively, gave to Mr. Dixon's work all the splendid setting that is deserved. Professor Netropid held the baton.

THE DRAMA.

Nanon" was presented, for the first time in this city, [the] Hollis Street Theatre on Monday night, be[fore] a very large audience. The libretto, by F. Zell, [i]s a very simple but fairly interesting story, which is [chi]efly concerned with the love of the lively innkeeper, [Nan]on, for the Marquis d'Aubigne, who, in the disguise [of] a regimental drummer, wins her heart, which has [resi]sted all previous attempts upon it. Believing the [int]entions of the supposed drummer to be honorable, [she] makes preparations for the signing of the marriage [con]tract in the presence of her relations and the villag[ers] generally, and suddenly, to his great surprise, he [find]s himself in a dilemma, from which, however, he [extr]icates himself by causing his own arrest for duel[ing]. The ceremonies are of course interrupted, and [Nan]on is left in despair. By and by the girl busies her[self] with attempting to secure the pardon of the false [cul]prit, and in the course of her efforts meets him in [his] proper person at the house of Ninon de l'Enclos. [He,] however, manages to deny his identity. Nanon at [len]gth secures a pardon for the drummer, and the Mar[qui]s, having by that time fought a real duel, and ren[der]ed himself liable to punishment, Nanon, who has [disc]overed his deception, frees him from danger by [givi]ng him the king's pardon. The Marquis repents, [and] takes Nanon to be his wife. The story, as will be [seen]s, is more interesting than German comic opera as [a] rule. There is an underplot in which a silly [nep]hew is tutored into the ways of the fashionable [wor]ld by a cunning old uncle who "knows it all," and [this] provides the fun of the book. It is not very bright [or v]ery diverting, and may be passed without further [con]sideration. The text has but little interest, and no [...]. The situations, however, are well contrived, and [the] constant movement of the piece prevents it from [bec]oming dull. It may also be credited with thorough [cle]anliness. The music is always gay and inspiriting. [It i]s nearly all in waltz and polka rhythms, but is in[var]iably pleasing. The waltz air which is the principal [the]me of the work is very graceful and pretty, and it [has] been used with much ingenuity, first in praise of [Nan]on, then to flatter Ninon, and finally, by the Abbe, to [com]pliment Mme. de Maintenon. In the last instance it [is c]leverly harmonized in the church style, and accom[pan]ied on the organ. The concerted numbers are ex[cell]ent, and the finales to the first and second acts are [unc]ommonly animated and effective. One of the most [com]mendable numbers in the opera, musically, is the [due]t between Nanon and the Marquis, in the second act, [and] the terzett between the three men in the last act is [sca]rcely less interesting.

[T]he performance was remarkably spirited from be[gin]ning to end. The acting in point of merit was [abo]ve the average to which we are accustomed in com[ed]ies of this description. The chorus was large and [san]g exceedingly well, and the orchestra, barring its [ten]dency to play over loud, especially the cornets, ac[qui]tted itself admirably. Mr. Carleton as the Marquis [san]g finely; in fact, almost as well as he ever did, and [his] acting was easy, animated and discreet throughout. [Mis]s Paullin, who played Nanon, acted with marked [ski]ll and cleverness, and with a quiet force and a simple [and] earnest truth to nature that were wholly winning. [She] sang, also, with intelligence and tunefulness, and [wit]h an artistic devotion to her task that went far to [ato]ne for a certain harshness of voice and lack of fin[ish] in style. It is rarely that so satisfying a perform[an]ce of the current comic opera heroine is vouchsafed. [Mis]s Alice Vincent made a very beautiful Nina, and [act]ed with a fair degree of skill, but her singing was [not] pleasing. Miss Wisdom was a picturesque Madame [de] Maintenon, and Miss Bartlett did very well with the [pa]rt of Gaston. Mr. C. H. Drew played the worldly [th]e Marquis de Marsillac with great vivacity and with [no] lack of genuine humor; but now and then he marred [his] efforts by a clownish exaggeration that neutralized [th]e effect of what was really artistic in his assump[tio]n. The silly nephew, Hector, was fairly and pleas[an]tly performed by Mr. Leumane, who has a very [sw]eet voice, which he uses with much neatness. He [m]ade one of the successes of the evening with his top[ica]l song, the encore verses of which were not only [not] superior to the generality of achievement in their [kin]d, but were witty and clever. Mr. Greensfelder's [Ab]be was, perhaps, lacking in ease and lightness of [sty]le, but his singing was very good, especially of the [son]g in the last act. The costumes were handsome, the [sce]nery was very pretty, especially that of the second [an]d last acts. In fact, the presentation of the opera as [a w]hole may be justly praised as one of the brightest [an]d most pleasing we have had here this season.

Hollis St. Theatre.

Between 781 Washington St. and 274 Tremont St.

ISAAC B. RICH, - - Proprietor and Manager.

COMMENCING MONDAY, APRIL 5, 1886.

Every Evening at 7.45, and Wednesday and Saturday Matinees at 2.

SECOND WEEK OF THE

CARLETON OPERA CO.

W. T. CARLETON PROPRIETOR AND MANAGER.

FROM THE CASINO, NEW YORK.

Production of the Great American and European Success,

"NANON,"

The Hostess of the Golden Lamb.

OPERA COMIQUE IN THREE ACTS, WITH

W. T. CARLETON,

And a Splendid Cast of Popular Metropolitan Artists,

Libretto, F. Zell. Music, R. Genee. Translation by Sydney Rosenfeld.

Produced under the direction of Mr. W. T. Carleton.

Cast of Characters:

NANON PATIN, Hostess of the Golden Lamb.......MISS LOUISE E. PAULLIN
NINON DE L'ENCLOS.......MISS ALICE VINCENT
MME. DE MAINTENON.......MISS CLARA WISDOM
GASTON, Page to Nanon.......MISS JOSEPHINE BARTLETT
JAQUELINE, Waitress.......MISS ROSE ALLEN
MME. DE FULPERT.......MISS ADA CLINTON
MLLE. D'ARMENONVILLE.......MISS E. SEYMOUR
MME. DE FRONTENAC.......MISS ETHEL CORLETT
COMTESSE HOULIERES.......MISS GEORGIE PETTIT
THERESE, Aunt of Nanon.......MISS MITA CAMERON
MARION.......MISS ANNIE MURRAY
PAGE OF MME. DE MAINTENON.......MISS JESSIE QUIGLEY
MARQUIS DE MARSILLAC.......MR. CHAS. H. DREW
HECTOR VICOMPTE DE MARSILLAC, Nephew of Marquis de Marsillac MR. C. M. LEUMANE
ABBE.......MR. JOS. S. GREENSFELDER
PIERRE.......MR. H. EHREND
SERGEANT.......MR. E. WALTERS
COMMISSIONER.......MR. ROLAND ROSS
NOTARY.......MR. H. DIXON
KING LOUIS XIV.......MR. TOM GUISE

—AND—

MARQUIS D'AUBIGNE. - MR. WM. T. CARLETON

Officers, Court Ladies and Gentlemen, Soldiers, Peasants, &c.

ACT I.—Inn of the Golden Lamb.—JOHN A. THOMPSON.
ACT II.—Salon of Ninon de L'Enclos.—JOHN A. THOMPSON.
ACT III.—Sanctuary of Mme. de Maintenon.—JOHN A. THOMPSON.

Stage Mechanism, ... By D. B. CRAIG AND ASSISTANTS
Properties, ... By WM. O'BRIEN AND ASSISTANTS
Calcium Effects, ... By FRED. A. CUTTER AND ASSISTANTS
Under the Supervision of MR. WM. DIXON, Stage Manager, Hollis St. Theatre.

Costumes from original designs by C. de Grimm, under the control of Mme. Loe.

MR. W. T. CARLETON'S STAFF.

Musical Director,	MR. F. INTROPIDI.	Acting Manager,	MR. TRACY TITUS.
Business Representative,	MR. A. H. CANBY.	Stage Manager,	MR. C. FAIR.

MATINEES WEDNESDAYS AND SATURDAYS AT 2.

Until Further Notice Doors Open at 1.30 and 7.15. Curtain Rises Promptly at 2 and 7.45.

gave out the dry, Frenchified maxims of living to his nephew Hector as if he had read Voltaire and "Le Sage" combined.

Mr. Fitzgerald's "Hector" was a good performance. The character was well dressed in the blue suit, not in the pink; and Mr. Fitzgerald has a fine, if rather a sharp, voice. He sang his couplet,

"I've concluded"

remarkably well, and will make an acquisition in future; in fact, a very good word should be said, that he helped to complete the cast most admirably. Mr. Herbert, as the Abbe in Madame Maintenon's reception room, was quaint and artistic. Miss Vincent could scarcely give enough "status" to the wonderful character she represented, and looked too young for Madame la Religieuse; but her dames d'honneur in their pious dresses were really exquisite. Mr. Standish as Pierre and Mr. Levick as the King personated their characters strongly; Louis XIV., that old rogue, was quite paternal in kissing Nanon, but he ought to have been made older, youth and middle age were gone with him when Madame de Maintenon ruled him.

I must say a word for Miss Billie Barlow, the beauty par excellence. First of all, Miss Barlow is such a pretty picture anywhere that she deserves to be dressed up in the best style possible, and her dress, outside of its scantiness, is not artistic. Blue plush, unless of a darker hue, kills. There are such loves of page dresses, such delights of white satin slashed with gold or crimson, that it needed not so peculiar a combination to make Miss Barlow look beautiful. Whoever designed the dress, should try again and do Miss Barlow justice.

As for the chorus, it was really good, and its sprightliness made up for all little mistakes. It did its work handsomely throughout, and put as much life into the scenes as possible. It was astonishing how well the performance went for a first night, and how steadily the orchestra supported under that excellent leader, Jesse Williams.

How is it, however, possible to give the readers of MUSIC AND DRAMA an idea of that sumptuousness which was applied to the whole mis-en-scene, of the clever minutiæ which was carried out in the whole piece; of that charming regiment of beautiful girls, who came on like tightly draped-Venuses, first with the "Drum, drum, drum," and then with flute and violin; of the brilliant ensemble, in fact, which has begun Messrs. Aronson's career in good earnest and has sprared neither time nor endeavor nor expense to give a bright and brilliant picture that amuses and pleases?

Put your stately criticism in your pocket, sir, and "thank the stars" that there is such a place as the Casino in New York, where they sing choruses like

"Uncles, nieces, aunts and cousins,"

Or,

"Oh, it's a proud po-ition,"

Or,

"See how he limps."

I am sure that "Nanon" wants no criticism to push it; it is so finely put on the stage that the brave little hostess of the "Golden Lamb" will for months push herself into the good graces of the New York public and encores and flowers will be showered down.

AMELIA LEWIS.

THE CASINO.

Production in English of "Nan[on]

The musical value of "Nanon" has been dis[cussed] and again since its production some months [at the] Thalia Theatre, and the principal airs are fam[iliar to the] ear of the public.

When the composer conceived the waltz m[elody] "Nanon, in rapture I come to thee," he well kn[ew he held] a trump card, and the only desire seems to ha[ve been to] play it as often as possible.

It was a happy example of dramatic superfet[ation, there]fore, which prompted the librettist to make thi[s melody] part and parcel of the plot. The most humorou[s and] only unique situations of the work are evolved out of this idea.

The "book" is the best translation presented of any of the German Comic operas, and seems doubly refreshing after the drivel which stood for the libretto of its predecessor "Polly."

The complaint heretofore has been that those performers who have successfully vocalized in comic opera, possess but slight acting talent.

The Messrs. Aronson had evidently inte[nded to reverse] these conditions, and give the public an ex[perience of a] cast mainly made up of performers with a [...] utation, but whose vocal qualities were lim[ited].

But as the voice is the vital ingredient of [opera, it] is at once seen how fatal such a policy migh[t be].

The sumptuous manner of its presentatio[n by the man]agement, however, completely filled the ey[e]. Such scenic splendor has not yet been view[ed in this thea]tre, and rarely in New York. After the lif[ting of the cur]tains on the second act, which represen[ts the salon of] *Ninon de L'Enclos*, the audience insisted up[on the appear]ance of the artist, Henry E. Hoyt. In colori[ng and treat]ment it was certainly a *chef d'œuvre* of sceni[c art].

The costumes were the richest ever show[n in any pro]duction in New York, and reflected great c[redit on the de]signer, C. De Grimm, the pictorial decorat[or of the *Gram*]*gram*.

In the first act the *figurantes*, to convey [the idea that] summer had but just come, wore a costume [of] berry, and in the second and third act, to fu[lly commem]orate the heated term, strawberry and va[nilla were the] chosen colors. Both of these designs were [...] and fitting *à la Jersey*, the effect was *showy* [...] scant. It is hoped that it is safe to say th[at never before] on our stage has the curve and contour of th[e female form] divine been exhibited in such unabashed lov[eliness].

Miss Sadie Martinot made her appearance as *Nanon*. Miss Martinot is one of the best so[ubrettes known to] the public, but she was deficient in vocal ab[ility. Her act]ing was arch and coquettish, withal a bit [...] the simple village maid, but altogether, c[...] acting stage needs Miss Martinot, and she l[acks the] voice to sing an occasional song which might legitimately fall to her. Miss Pauline H[all] sang the music in satisfying [...] *Gaston*, page to *Ninon*, wore [...] blue satin and pink ostrich [...] singing out of tune. W. [...] *D'Aubigne* seemed to feel th[e ...] sang with good judgment an[d ...] chance Mr. W. H. Fitzgera[ld's] singing of the really cleve[r ...] question of Time." The re[...] vein. The words were give[n ...] till the stock of verses ran o[ut ...] small bit successfully and i[...] has a good voice and should [...]

Joe Jefferson and Old Co[...] from their fishing excursion [...] they heard that Wm. Herbe[rt ...] music of the *Abbé* even a little bit. Gustavus Levick played *King Louis XIV.*, by special arrangement. It seemed so. Francis Wilson squeezed all the humor out of the *Marquis de Marsillac* the part afforded. New business will doubtless be added as the opera runs on. The heartiest applause of the evening greeted his rendering of "I am an Impressario."

The drilling of the chorus and the stage business was almost perfect in its detail, and Herr Conried was led to the footlights and presented with a wreath. Manager Aronson was loudly called for, but did not appear.

The production of "Nanon" was virtually the opening under the new *régime* at the Casino. And in the lavishness of its presentment the public have a proof of all that was promised. It is a pleasure to be able to congratulate the Messrs. Aronson on the success in its entirety of their first venture, and to predict a long run for "Nanon."

REAL FIG[...] THE STAGE.

Fraulein Gro[...]es to Assume th[e] [...] Page.

[Special [...] Boston Herald.]

NEW YORK, [...]. Fraulein Gros[...] one of the mo[...] the Thalia Theat[re] company, appe[...] the stage yesterd[ay] to assist in [...] of "Nanon." When she dis[covered] that she had bee[n] assigned to the [...] page she became very indignant [...] refused to accept [...] Manager Amb[erg] told her that sh[e] must sing the [...] the prima donna. [...] sponded by [...] the music [...] his feet, [...] and, Emil [...] advanced [...] Mr. Amb[erg] in a threatenin[g ...] and, when the [...] hands interfe[...] general scuffle ensu[ed ...] Finally, Mr. M[...] [...]ffs were taken to [the] station by a po[liceman ...] Mr. Amberg declin[ed] to prosecute th[em ...] they were released.

The Thalia Theatre.

Energy and enterprise have long been two of the most prominently noticeable characteristics displayed by the management of the Thalia. It was here that the opera of "Nanon," which has since been so exceedingly successful and popular, was first brought out, and many other attractive plays and operettas have, like this one, first been presented to the public in this theatre. A large corps of artists is continually ready to be called upon. All of them are versatile, and for this reason the possibility of giving a wide range of pieces is greatly increased. Every principal actor is gifted with an easy confidence and a dignified presence and possessed of ripe experience, so that each commands not only the admiration, but the respect of his audience. Last evening many favorites were in the cast. Fräulein Raberg as *Ninon de l'Enclos* was a stately and brilliant figure, her social attainments in the art of singing being clearly perceptible even in the rather small musical part that falls to her lot in the operetta. Max Lube as the *Intendant* was amusing, though with a kind of compulsory gayety that cast a slight shadow over the scene. Herr Edouard Elsbach made a clearly defined and always consistent picture of the foppish nephew, and both in acting and singing was eminently good.

Fräulein Emmy Meffert, the *Nanon*, is a charming little actress and a sweet singer, and she showed great vivacity, a large amount of jolly fun, and many of the nods and becks and other regulation gesticulations of the furthest opera bouffe school. There was no pretence about her love making, and nothing left to the imagination. The *Marquis d'Aubigne* (Herr Schütz) said with mournful and earnest pathos a sentence occurring in his lines, "I am completely torn in pieces," after a series of embraces which *Nanon* showered upon him in quick succession. Fräulein Meffert's voice is both pleasing and powerful.

This evening "Der Freischütz" will be given, on Wednesday the "Bettelstudent," and on Friday Herr Ferdinand Wachtel makes his first appearance.

MUSIC AND THE DRAMA.

A NEW OPERETTA.

"Nanon," an operetta from the pens of those tireless co-workers, Zell and Genee, was produced at the Thalia Theatre, in the Bowery, on Friday night. Its reception was so cordial that last night seats were not to be had after the curtain rose on the first act, and the audience followed the clever German comedians through the play with the greatest attention, and frequent bursts of laughter and applause testified the keenness of their enjoyment.

The operetta is not new in Germany, where it achieved one of the notable successes of last year, but we believe this was the first representation in this country. It is the twelfth work of the kind which Mr. Amberg has placed on his list since he became manager of the Thalia and it is pleasant to record that his enterprise and earnestness of purpose bid fair to meet with the reward they merit in a long and prosperous run of his latest novelty.

"Nanon" has the advantage over many of its companion operettas of the Viennese school of a remarkably clever libretto. For their plot Messrs. Zell and Genee, as they have done before, went to a French comedy, and they have interwoven dialogue and music in so skilful a manner that one element seems to give [illegible] to the other. The ingenious dramatic [illegible] of which the piece is full, are matched by equally ingenious musical conceits, of which the crowning one is the [illegible] of a single song by three different characters, which goes through appropriate transformations, and finally emerges as a pious canticle aimed to promote the pious meditations of *Madame de Maintenon*. Pretty melodies abound in the work, the stately minuet is effectively used, and if the skill of a Strauss had been applied to the instrumentation the operetta would rival the best of the famous dance composer's creations in this department of music. The representation by Mr. Amberg's people is well-balanced and spirited, and the comedy is handsomely mounted.

The story hinges upon the gallantry of the *Marquis d'Aubigne*, the favored lover for the moment of *Ninon de l'Enclos*, and his adventure with *Nanon Patin*, the young and beautiful hostess of the Golden Lamb inn, which is brought to a happy termination after a series of lively incidents and amusing situations. In wooing the hostess the *Marquis*, who is masquerading as a drummer, *Grignan*, introduces the serenade to *Anna*, which so charms the *Marquis de Marsillac*, who overhears it, that he makes complete notes of it. *D'Aubigne*, when confronted with the prospect of being married to Nanon, escapes through a pretended arrest made by his friends. *Nanon* seeks the assistance of *Ninon* to relieve her lover from his supposed incarceration and subsequently both women are led to ask the intercession of *Madame de Maintenon* with *Louis XIV.*, the one for her lover, the supposed drummer, and the other for her lover, the *Marquis*, who has meantime been involved in a duel with the *Vicomte de Marsillac* growing out of the latter's devotion to both *Nanon* and *Ninon*. A lucky chance throws *Nanon* in the way of the *King*, whom she calls with charming ingenuousness *Monsieur The Maintenon*, and who is so pleased with her grace that he grants full pardon to her lover. It requires only this favor done by his faithful sweetheart to win *d'Aubigne's* heart completely and he makes amends for his former desertion by redeeming the vows of the pseudo drummer.

* * *

The demand for seats at the Casino has been so active since the production of "Nanon" that the management have arranged to book seats four weeks ahead. The popularity of this opera is not a matter of such great surprise to me, considering that it has run over 400 nights in Berlin, and is still being played with great success in Hamburg, Leipzig, Hanover, Prague, Bremen, Dresden and other European cities. The libretto by Zell has fortunately not been butchered in the translation. The plot is unusually original, and is a delightful exception in this respect to most of the comic operas that have been produced recently in New York. The argument is as follows:

Nanon is the hostess of an inn before the gates of Paris, called, "The Golden Lamb," which has gained renown alike by a casual visit of *Louis XIV.* and *Nanon's* reputation for beauty and virtue. On this account, *Marsillac*, director of the royal theatre, takes his nephew *Hector*, an inexperienced country nobleman, to see *Nanon*. At the same time the famous beauty, *Ninon de l'Enclos*, also pays a visit to the "Golden Lamb" to secretly get a sight of her rival, as she has become suspicious that her lover, the *Marquis d'Aubigne*, has turned his affections towards *Nanon*. But there, she hears that *Nanon* is going to be married to the drummer *Grignan* on the same day, and returns appeased. This drummer *Grignan* is no other than the *Marquis d'Aubigne*, who, under this disguise, intends to abduct the beautiful hostess. The evening before her birthday he, together with his pretended comrades, a drummer and piper of the regiment, sings her a serenade: "Anna, in rapture I come to thee." She surprises him with a proposal of marriage, when the notary, the relatives of *Nanon* and the wedding guests make their appearance, *d'Aubigne* causes himself to be arrested by his colonel on account of a duel. In the midst of her grief *Nanon* receives a ring and friendly compliments from *Gaston*, the page of *Ninon de l'Enclos*, and she concludes to pray that lady to help her in rescuing *Grignan*, as by the command of the king dueling is punishable with death.

The second act shows the salon of *Ninon* on a ball night. Here are met *Marsillac*, *Hector*, and a gallant abbé, who is one of *Ninon's* lovers, and at the same time confessor of *Mme. de Maintenon*. *D'Aubigne* likewise appears, joyfully received by *Ninon*, and when she reproaches him for having stayed away so long and for having forgotten her birthday, he draws himself out of his embarrassment by singing her the same serenade, "Anna, in rapture I come to thee." Soon afterward *Nanon* arrives to ask for *Ninon's* help in saving *Grignan's* life. *Hector* and *d'Aubigne* also meet the latter, doubly jealous, that *Hector* pays court to *Ninon* as well as to *Nanon*, challenges him and both hurry into *Ninon's* garden to decide their quarrel with swords. Meantime *Marsillac* has prepared a surprise for *Ninon;* he has noted the serenade of *Grignan* and now pays his homage to her by singing, accompanied by the musicians of the court chapel, "Anna, in rapture I come to thee." However, he is laughed at by *Ninon* and her company; *d'Aubigne* returns from his duel and he is asked to clear up the origin

of the song; but
guard which ent
have been seen. I
in the hip, refuse
excites the humo
he limps about, t

The third act
Maintenon, whos
to her in the sha
mien the serena
come to thee."
freedom, and rec
the nephew of *M*
D'Aubigne congr
day with the sam
so that the merr
anew. *Ninon* an
de Maintenon, to
d'Aubigne and *G*
non as a presen
the pardon to *Ni*
now recognizes
nanimity *Grigna*
by the sudden fa
sent, and the h
Marquise d'Aubi

The performan
first night. Miss
in her nondescrip
taken. This do
vocally, and nov
got his voice und
of his rôle with k
Keynote in givi
Abbé, vice Wm.
been made and h
ing nightly encor
waltz song to the
Francis Wilson's d
so distinctly that
voice. New com
part has been elal
list of successes v
the house. Miss

larly pleasing in quality, has so much improved of late that she deserves great credit for the study of which this is the result. Her waltz song, introduced in the third act, is well rendered. W. H. Fitzgerald is adding new verses to his topical song, "Only a Question of Time," and discarding those which prove ineffective. I would suggest to him that the words "lad*en*" and "maid*en*," which occur in the first verse, are not pronounced laid-*on* and made-*on*. The scenic effects are received with the same admiration—the minor characters and the chorus show the watchful eye of Herr Conried. The costumes of the *figurantes* are descanted on by the audiences and have really proved one of the best advertisements for the piece.

* * *

In a conversation with Edward Aronson that gentleman said that what was aimed at most of all was a harmonious entirety in the production of "Nanon," and every member of the cast was selected to achieve that end.

What is more stupid in comic opera than a woman who cannot act, no matter how phenomenal her voice may be.

The combination of a great voice and acting talent is not yet discovered in comic opera. Théo, Aimée and Judic never possessed remarkable singing voices, and yet the French accepted them as exemplars of opera bouffe, when many of the actresses in their own companies playing minor parts could discount them vocally. It is not contended that Miss Martinot has a remarkable voice, but in presence and performance she is the best representative of *Nanon* that possibly could have been secured.

Last Sunday evening the Mexican editors were present by invitation of Rudolph Aronson at the concert on the Casino Roof Garden. The national colors of Mexico were displayed and the national air was played in honor of the visitors. The large audience applauded as the visitors entered.

"The Mikado" is announced for production at the Union Square Theatre next Monday by Sidney Rosenfeld's Opera Company, barring injunctions and other calamities which, like "My Grandfather's Clock," may cause the enterprise to "stop short, never to go again." I am told that both Stetson and McCaull are "laying low" for Sidney's scalp. But then the threats of managers are apt to partake of more bark than bite.

ELLERY BERG.

SADIE MARTINOT AS NANON.

Not a week ago, as Miss Sadie Martinot, the popular Nanon at the Casino, was about to assume her role on the stage, she received a message from the proprietor of a theatrical newspaper called the *Stage*. He had an article which before publishing he wished to submit to her. The stage rules at the Casino under Mr. Conried's management are very strict and it is impossible to get admission to the performers during the play. Miss Martinot, therefore, had to wait until the performance was over before hearing what the editor of the *Stage* had to say. She then met in the hotel parlor opposite and in the presence of a friend the agent who had been sent to her. He gave her the manuscript of the article referred to and she read it through. It spoke of her personal relations to men connected with the press, used in a most unwarrantable manner the names of well-known men and managed to convey the idea that the criticisms of Miss Martinot's Nanon were all influenced favorably or otherwise by her personal treatment of the writers.

The actress threw up her hands after running through the article. "In the name of heaven," she cried, "you do not intend to publish any such infamous and injurious rubbish as this, do you?"

The agent did not see how it could be prevented. He had an idea that it was a very nice article. Miss Martinot then gave him back his manuscript and went away in great distress. "O, dear, I'll pay anything rather than have that stuff printed about me," she said. "I cannot bear the idea of being thought such an idiot."

The next day a friend was sent to the office of the *Stage* to see if the obnoxious stuff could not be kept out of print. The man in the office did not see how it could be done. Then the friend of Miss Martinot said they were willing to pay to keep it out. The man thought it might be arranged. Notes now began to arrive at the Casino from Mr. Barker Bradford, the editor of the *Stage*. The first one reads as follows:

PRIVATE OFFICE OF BARKER BRADFORD,
542 Broadway, June 30.

MISS MARTINOT: Will you kindly send me word where I may send a reporter to interview you and obtain your picture? I intend to present you with a front page portrait. Very truly, BARKER BRADFORD,
Editor and Proprietor of the *Stage*.

No notice was taken of this, and the next day Miss Martinot received the following:

[...] mail Miss Martinot. We object to it. If you don't stop it at this point we'll arrest you. We can't have her annoyed any more."

Mr. Bradford was profuse in explanations, and said he only intended to "puff" the lady.

"One word more," said Mr. Aronson. "Just come in here and write a note to Miss Martinot."

Once in the office, Mr. Bradford wrote in the presence of the detective the following note:

DEAR MISS MARTINOT: I have seen Mr. Aronson, and you need not fear anything. The article is destroyed and will not appear. BARKER BRADFORD.

On the 11th of July Miss Martinot received the following letter

DEAR MISS MARTINOT: According to promise I have destroyed the papers that were printed. I have unlocked the forms and distributed the type and notified the American News Company that the paper will not appear until Wednesday of next week. Now will you grant me the favor of loaning me $50 for ten days, when I will repay you with good interest? This will quite smooth things, and the delay in the paper will not embarrass me in the least, for that amount will answer for that which the paper would bring in if it came out to-day. Most faithfully, BARKER BRADFORD.

Inclosed in this letter was a promissory note, of which the following is a fac-simile:

July 11, 1885
I agree to keep out of my paper an article which Miss Sadie Martinot objects to being put in print and further agree to pay her within ten days from date 50 dollars borrowed money.
Barker Bradford

In a short interview with Sadie Martinot yesterday she said that she had not advanced the $50. She was not acquainted with Bradford, and was chiefly indignant that such "infamous rubbish" as imputed to her in the threatened article should be put into her mouth. Miss Martinot is an intelligent woman without squeamishness, and appears to be sincerely distressed at the whole occurrence.

As an exemplification of the strange newspaper methods employed with actresses this occurence is not without its value.

Dec 1883

....The new three-act buffo opera "Nanon," with music by Richard Genée, is far superior to the general run of the more recent works belonging to the same category, and is drawing large houses to the Walhalla-Operetten-Theatre, Berlin, where it was recently produced. On the first night several pieces had to be repeated. The principal singers were called on after each act, as were also Herr Genée himself, Herr Pleininger, the conductor, and Herr Grosskopf, the proprietor of the theatre, after the second act, and at the fall of the curtain for the last time.

"Nanon" at the Thalia.

Genée's latest operetta, "Nanon," which is said to have had a great success in Germany, was last evening [illegible] at the Thalia Theatre before a crowded [illegible], and won a popular success. Although none of its numbers can be compared with the best things in the works of Strauss and Suppé, there are several songs which may win a succès de boudoir. The libretto is fairly entertaining and the leading rôles were satisfactorily rendered by Frl. Meffert, Frau Raberg, Herren Liebe, Elsach, and Schütz. Jan 3/85

Walhalla-Operetten-Theater.

Sonntag: Zum 305. Male:

Nanon.

Operette in 3 Akten, frei nach einem Lustspiele der Herren Theaulon und d'Artois von F. Zell u. Rich. Genée. Musik von Rich. Genée.
Kassenöffnung 6 Uhr Anfang 7 Uhr Ende 9½ Uhr.
Montag: Dieselbe Vorstellung.

CALIFORNIA.

A SCENE NOT DOWN IN THE BILLS

Sheriff Prevented From Serving an Injunction on "Nanon."

SAN FRANCISCO, Sept. 8.—Leo Goldmark and Henri Conrad, owners of the copyright of the opera "Nanon," obtained an injunction yesterday to prevent the production of the opera at the Tivoli, a family resort, owned by Kreling Brothers. A deputy sheriff went to the Tivoli, and attempted to go behind the scenes in search of the proprietors, on whom he desired to serve the papers. He was stopped by attaches, and drew a revolver to force his way to the stage, but was quickly disarmed, and summarily ejected from the building. Later the sheriff made efforts to serve the injunction papers, but without success, and the opera was produced without interruption.

CALIFORNIA.

The "Nanon" Injunction Case.

Opera Managers Fined and Imprisoned.

SAN FRANCISCO, Sept. 9.—Joseph N. Kreling, one of the proprietors of the Tivoli Opera House, where "Nanon" was produced Monday night, despite the injunction granted by Judge Reardon, was yesterday convicted of contempt of court, fined $500, and sentenced to imprisonment in the county jail for five days. John and William Kreling, brothers of Joseph and past-proprietors of the Tivoli, were each fined $250 and sentenced to imprisonment for two days.

RUDOLPH ARONSON, ... MANAGER.

Every Evening at 8. Saturday Matinee at 2

Programme for the Week ending August 9, 1885.

"NANON"

THE HOSTESS OF

"THE GOLDEN LAMB."

OPERA COMIQUE IN THREE ACTS.

Libretto F. ZELL. Music R. GENEE.

Translation by SYDNEY ROSENFELD.

Produced under the direction of Mr. HEINRICH CONRIED.

—CAST OF CHARACTERS.—

NANON PATIN, Hostess of the Golden Lamb,........SADIE MARTINOT
NINON DE L'ENCLOS,........PAULINE HALL
GASTON, Page to Ninon,........BILLIE BARLOW
MME. DE MAINTENON,........ALICE VINCENT
JAQUELINE, Waitress,........AGNES FOLSOM
MME. DE FULPERT,........ROSE BEAUDET
MLLE. D'ARMENONVILLE,........CARRIE ANDREWS
MME. DE FRONTENAC,........FLORENCE BELL
COMTESSE HOULIERES,........ADELAIDE LANGDON
THERESE, Aunt of Nanon,........MARIE KOENIG
LISETTE,........SADIE WELLS
MARION,........EMMA HANLEY
PAGE OF MME. DE MAINTENON,........CLARA WISDOM
MARQUIS D'AUBIGNE, (Specially Engaged.)......WM. T. CARLETON
HECTOR VICOMPTE DE MARSILLAC, Nephew of Marquis de Marsillac, WM. H. FITZGERALD
ABBE,........ALEXIS MARKHAM
PIERRE,........HARRY STANDISH
BOMBARDINI, Drum-Major,........C. L. WEEKS
SERGEANT,........G. T. WADE
COMMISSIONER,........J. McDOWELL
NOTARY,........O. HEILIG

AND

MARQUIS DE MARSILLAC,........FRANCIS WILSON

AND

KING LOUIS XIV, (by special arrangement)......GUSTAVUS LEVICK

Officers, Court Ladies and Gentlemen, Soldiers, Peasants, &c.

SYNOPSIS OF SCENERY.

ACT I.—Inn of the Golden Lamb—JNO. MAZZANOVICH.
ACT II.—Salon of Ninon de L'Enclos—HENRY E. HOYT.
ACT III.—Sanctuary of Mme. de Maintenon—HARLEY MERRY.

*** NOTE.—Intermission of fifteen minutes between Acts I and II, and ten minutes between Acts II and III. The words of the Topical Song in Act II are by Messrs. HARLEY & HAUSER.

Costumes under the supervision of Mme. Loe from original designs by C. DE GRIMM.

Stage Director, - HEINRICH CONRIED	Stage Machinist, G. P. SHERWOOD, Jr
Music Director, - - JESSE WILLIAMS	Properties, - - W. M. HOLLOHAN
Stage Manager, - W. H. FITZGERALD	Gas Machinist, - - JAS. McGOVERN

The Antique Carved Furniture and Bric-a-brac used in this Opera, are from the establishment of H. B. Herts & Sons, 142 Fifth Avenue.

The WEBER PIANO used here. | The MASON & HAMLIN ORGAN used here.

All the music performed at this theatre may be obtained (if published) at Pond's Music Store, 25 Union Square, N. Y.

Ladies' Toilet Rooms at head of Balcony Stairs. Gentlemen's Toilet Room on Balcony Floor

CAFE AND SMOKING ROOM DOWN STAIRS.

Edward Aronson says that the receipts for the first fifty performances of "Nanon" at the New York Casino amounted to $50,000, or an average of $1000 a night. This makes the opera the most successful since the opening of the house.

("Die Wirthin vom goldnen Lamm")

KOMISCHE OPER

in drei Acten

von F. Zell und Richard Genée.

MUSIK VON

RICHARD GENÉE.

Vollstandiger Clavierauszug mit Text Pr. M. 12. — / fl. 6. 30.

Clavierauszug ohne Text Pr. M. 4. 50 / fl. 2. 70.

London, Ent. Sta. Hall.

Verlag von Aug. Cranz in Hamburg.

Wien, C. A. Spina
Verlags u. Kunsthandlung (Alwin Cranz)

Brüssel, A. Cranz.

It is probably but little known that Genée's operetta of "Nanon," when produced for the first time in Vienna, about ten years ago, was a failure. Either the public taste has changed since then, or else that verdict was a mistake, for I see that the Walhalla theatre alone, in Berlin, has paid the composer royalties amounting to £1500, to say nothing of what he has received from Magdeburg, Leipzig, and Breslau, where the piece has been and still is a favourite. 1884

—The first act of "Nanon," which is to be brought out at the New York Casino next Monday night, Miss Sadie Martinot as Nanon will feed doves, while pigs, geese, goats and other live stock will wander about, and the entrance of farmers, with other live specimens as wedding presents, will be the decidedly realistic feature of the performance.

"NANON."

The following is the story of "Nanon," Richard opera, which was recently produced at the New-Yorl it is now running to crowded houses nightly: —

Nanon is the hostess of an inn before the gates The Golden Lamb, which has gained renown alike b of Louis XIV. and by Nanon's reputation for bea On this account, Marsillac, director of the Royal Th nephew, Hector, an inexperienced country nobleman At the same time the famous beauty, Ninon de l'Enc visit to The Golden Lamb to secretly get a sight of l has become suspicious that her lover, the Marquis turned his affections toward Nanon. But there Nanon is going to be married to the drummer, Grign day, and returns appeased. This drummer, Grignat than the Marquis d'Aubigne, who, under this disg abduct the beautiful hostess. The evening before h together with his pretended comrades, a drummer an regiment, sings her a serenade: "Anna, in Rapt Thee." She surprises him with a proposal of marria notary, the relatives of Nanon, and the wedding gu appearance, D'Aubigne causes himself to be arrested on account of a duel. In the midst of her grief, Nanon receives a ring and friendly compliments from Gaston, the page of Ninon de l'Enclos, and she concludes to pray that lady to help her in rescuing Grignan, as, by the command of the King, dueling is punishable with death.

The second act shows the salon of Ninon on a ball night. Here are met Marsillac, Hector, and a gallant Abbe, who is one of Ninon's lovers, and at the same time confessor of Madame de Maintenon. D'Aubigne likewise appears, joyfully received by Ninon; and when she reproaches him for having staid away so long, and for having forgotten her birthday, he draws himself out of his embarrassment by singing her the same serenade, "Anna, in Rapture I come to Thee." Soon afterward Nanon arrives to ask for Ninon's help in saving Grignan's life. Hector and D'Aubigne also meet. The latter, doubly jealous, that Hector pays court to Ninon as well as to Nanon, challenges him, and both hurry into Ninon's garden to decide their quarrel with swords. Meantime Marsillac has prepared a surprise for Ninon. He has noted the serenade of Grignan, and now pays his homage to her by singing, accompanied by the musicians of the court chapel, "Anna, in Rapture I come to Thee." However, he is laughed at by Ninon and her company. D'Aubigne returns from his duel, and is asked to clear up the origin of the song; but he is prevented from doing this by the guard which enters at the same moment. The duelists have been seen. Hector, who has been wounded by a thrust in the hip, refuses to give the name of his opponent, and excites the humor of the company by the ridiculous way in which he limps about, whereupon he is led away a prisoner.

The third act leads us into the sanctuary of Madame de Maintenon, whose name is Anna also; and the Abbe sings to her, in the shape of a pious hymn, and with hypocritical mien, the serenade of the drummer: "Anna, in Rapture I come to Thee." Marsillac appears, to ask for his nephew's freedom, and receives it, the fact appearing that D'Aubigne, the nephew of Madame de Maintenon, is the challenging party. D'Aubigne congratulates her on the occasion of her birthday with the same Anna song, and Marsillac after him, so that the merry war over the origin of the song arises anew. Ninon and Nanon both request audience with Madame de Maintenon, to pray for grace for their respective lovers, D'Aubigne and Grignan. Nanon receives the life of Grignan as a present from the King, and she in turn presents the pardon to Ninon, in order to save D'Aubigne, whom she now recognizes as Grignan. Touched by so much magnanimity, Grignan offers her his hand. Maintenon, disquieted by the sudden favor of the King for Nanon, gives her consent, and the hostess of The Golden Lamb is made Marquise d'Aubigne.

"Nanon" had its first American production in English at the Casino, New York, under Rudolph Aronson's management, June 29, and made an immediate hit with both press and public. The Brooklyn *Eagle* says that it "will run until the snow falls again" The cast is an especially fine one, the following people appearing in the principal parts: —

NANON PATIN, Hostess of The Golden Lamb........SADIE MARTINOT
NINON DE L'ENCLOS........PAULINE HALL
GASTON, Page to Ninon........BILLEE BARLOW
MADAME DE MAINTENON........ALICE VINCENT
JAQUELINE, Waitress........AGNES FOLSOM
MADAME DE FULPERT........ROSE BEAUDET
M'LLE D'ARMENONVILLE........CARRIE ANDREWS
MADAME DE FRONTENAC........FLORENCE BELL
COMTESSE BOULIERES........ADELAIDE LANGDON
THERESE, Aunt of Nanon........MARIE KOENIG
LISETTE........ADIE WELLS
MARION........EMMA HANLEY
PAGE OF MADAME DE MAINTENON........CLARA WISDOM
MARQUIS D'AUBIGNE........WILLIAM T. CARLETON
HECTOR VICOMTE DE MARSILLAC........WILLIAM H. FITZGERALD
ABBE........WILLIAM HERBERT
PIERRE........HARRY STANDISH
BOMBARDINI, Drum-Major........ALEXIS MARKHAM
SERGEANT........G. T. WADE
COMMISSIONER........C. L. WEEKS
NOTARY........O. HELLIG
MARQUIS DE MARSILLAC........FRANCIS WILSON
KING LOUIS XIII........GUSTAVUS LEVICK

Brilliant Performance and Assemblage at the Pretty Casino.

Last night was indeed a gala night at the Casino, and the beautiful theatre was crowded to its utmost capacity, the occasion being the 100th representation of Richard Genée's popular and sparkling opera-comique of "Nanon." Not a one was every seat in the house taken, but throngs of spectators stood in the [illegible] the stage [illegible]

The house itself presented a holiday appearance, tastefully decorated as it was with flowers and [illegible]. Every [illegible] with a souvenir [illegible] book [illegible] the [illegible] of the opera [illegible] Casino on the cover. It also contained portraits of the principals in the cast.

[illegible] Mr. W. T. Carleton [illegible] costume [illegible] Miss Pauline Hall [illegible] made of black satin [illegible] Mr. Carleton received a large wreath [illegible] Among the audience were such distinguished personages as Chauncey Depew, [illegible] John Boyle [illegible] Mr. Le Roy, [illegible] and other well-known people.

After the performance the usual [illegible] concert was given, Rudolph Aronson's fine orchestra furnishing the music. [illegible] in the person of [illegible] Rudolph Aronson's [illegible] "My Darling"

"Nanon" is the [illegible] at the Casino [illegible] of Rudolph Aronson, and [illegible] All the [illegible] run of [illegible] 200 nights for this [illegible] opera.

There will be another gala night at the Casino next Monday evening [illegible]

(„Die Wirthin vom goldnen Lamm")

KOMISCHE OPER

in drei Acten

von F. Zell und Richard Genée.

MUSIK VON

RICHARD GENÉE.

Vollständiger Clavierauszug mit Text Pr. M. 12.— fl. 6. 30.

Clavierauszug ohne Text Pr. M. 4. 50 fl. 2. 70.

London, Ent. Sta. Hall.

Verlag von Aug. Cranz in Hamburg.

Wien, C. A. Spina Verlags u. Kunsthandlung (Alwin Cranz)

Brüssel, A. Cranz.

C

RECENT DEATHS.

The Composer of "Nanon."

Richard Genee, the composer and librettist, who has just died at Vienna, will be best remembered in this country as the composer of "Nanon." He was born at Davtzig on Feb. 7, 1823. Drifting into a musical career early in life, in 1848 he became the musical director of the opera house at Revel, and from that time had been successively director of the theatres or opera houses of Riga, of Cologne, of Aix-la-Chapelle, of Dusseldorf, of Mayence, of Dantzig, of Schwerin, of Prague, and of the An der Wien in Vienna. Genee first became known as a writer of songs and choruses of a humorous character. He wrote the words for these songs as he afterwards wrote the librettos for his own operas and for many of those of Strauss, Von Suppé, and Millöcker. Genee's first comic opera, in three acts, "Rosita," was produced at Mayence in 1864, and was received with much enthusiasm. This encouraged him and soon after he wrote an operetta, the "Enemy of Music," which was played at Vienna. In 1868 the opera "Am Runenstein," in which F. de Flotow collaborated with him, was produced at Prague, but proved a flat failure. In 1876 he again achieved success with "Der See-Cadet," which was produced in Vienna, and has been the most popular of his operas in Europe. In 1877 followed "Nanon;" "The Last of the Mohicans" in 1878; "Nisida" in 1880, which proved even more popular in Vienna than "Der See-Cadet;" and many others. "The Royal Middy," which has had long runs in this country, is an adaptation of "Der See-Cadet." Richard Genee's younger brother, Rudolph Genee, is a well-known German dramatist and dramatic critic.

um 15. Juni. 1895

Fritz Luckhardt, in Wien.

NANON. A Comic Opera in three acts by Genee. Oct. 2. 1896

MARQUIS DE MARSELLAC	Mr. OSCAR GIRARD
HECTOR DE MARSELLAC, his nephew	Mr. EDWARD TEMPLE
MARQUIS HENRI D'AUBUGNE, the King's chamberlain	Mr. J. K. MURRAY
BOMBARDINI, his henchman	Mr. LINDSAY MORISON
LOUIS XIV	Mr. STANLEY FELCH
MONS. L'ABBE	Mr. W. H. CLARKE
THE NOTARY	J. C. DEAN
NANON, Mistress of the Golden Lamb	Miss CLARA LANE
NINON DE L'ENCLOS	Miss LAURA MILLARD
MME. DE FRONTENAC	Miss ADDIE NORWOOD
COUNTESS HONLIERS	Miss BERTHA LEHMAN
GASTON, Ninon's Page	Miss HATTIE BELLE LADD
MME. DE MAINTENON, the King's [illegible]	Miss ROSE LEIGHTON
COUSIN PIERRE, (Nanon's Country Relations)	Mr. CHARLES SCRIBNER
UNCLE MATTHEW (Nanon's Country Relations)	Mr. BRITTON STEPHENS
COUSIN JOE (Nanon's Country Relations)	Mr. ALEXANDER J. JOEL
PAPA BERTRAND (Nanon's Country Relations)	CHAS. M. HOLLY
MOTHER LIZETTE (Nanon's Country Relations)	Miss CORA SCRIBNER
AUNT THERESA (Nanon's Country Relations)	Miss IDA CLARKE
COUSIN MARION (Nanon's Country Relations)	Miss GEORGIANA DELAND
BAPTISTE, Nun	Miss HATTIE BELLE LADD
ARMANDE, Nun	Miss BERTHA DAVIS

Chorus of Peasants, Soldiers, Country Relations, Courtiers, Ladies, Etc.

SYNOPSIS OF SCENERY.

ACT I—The Golden Lamb.

ACT II.—Ninon's Salon.

ACT III.—Boudoir of Mme. de Maintenon.

Ouverture.

Richard Genée.

C. 26020.

Allegretto.

f
ff
fz
fz
ff
decres.
p
ff
p
decresc.

Allegretto un poco moderato.
dol.
p
f
f
ff
sf
Un poco meno mosso.
p
mf

rallent.
a tempo.
Tempo I.
rall.
cresc.

Allegretto.
G.P.
Molto vivace.
cresc.

piu cresc.
f
ff
1.
2.
p
p
cresc.
f
ff

Nº 1. Introduction.

Wein, den schenkt sie uns ein! Da - rum ist auch weithin in
köst-lichsten Wein schenkt sie ein!
Stadt und in Land die-ses Hänschen von Nanon be-liebt und be-kannt. Da lebt sich's char-
mant, da lebt sich's char - mant, da lebt sich's da lebt sich's char-mant; ___ und
lebt sich's, da lebt sich's char- mant! ___

wenn sie ein Lied_chen er - klin_gen uns lässt, das ist ein Fest!
Und wenn sie ein Liedchen er - klin_gen lässt das ist ein
Das ist ein Fest! Auch vorneh_me Herrn kom_men oft her und gern, denn Na_non,
Fest!
Na_non, heis_set ihr Stern, ja Na_non, Na_non heis_set ihr Stern!

Allegro.
Hoch,
Da ist sie,
Da kommt sie!
Allegro.
mf
cresc.
f
Nanon.
Meno mosso.
Dan - ke, Dan - ke, lie-ben
Na - non hoch, Na-non hoch, Na-non hoch!
Meno mosso.
N
Leu - te, Freunde, Nachbar'n, Dank! Doch wess-halb tönt heu - te
mir ein sol-cher Sang! Ei mor-gen ist Sanct An-nentag, da muss man heut schon gratu -
Corporal.

C
li - ren!
Nanon
Wie
Sanct An - nen - tag! Sanct An - nen - tag!
f
f
p
N
muss mich so viel Freundschaft rüh - ren. Ob er an diesen Tag gedacht wohl haben
rall.
rall.
rall.
rall.
mag.
Allegro.
Hoch Na - non, ih - re Rei - ze, ih - re Lie - der und ihr Wein, sie be -
f
f
f
Allegro.
f

geistern, sie ent_zü_cken Alt und Jung, Alt und Jung, Gross und Klein!
Corporal (Nanon einen Blumenstrauss überreichend.)
Was Eu_er Herz be_geh_ren mag ward Euch er_
füllt am heut'_ gen Tag.
Doch Eu_re lieb_ sten
Wünsche nennt uns hier!
Nanon.
Was ich mir wün_ sche, fra_ get
Ihr? Was ich mir wün_ sche fra_get Ihr?

Allegro con spirito.
f
decresc.
Nanon.
Mein
p
freund_liches Wirtshaus um_rankt ist's von Wei_ne; die Trauben sie rei_fen im
Son_nenschein; ge_füllt ist's mit Gästen im fro_hem Ver_ei_ne; was
f
colla parte.
p
kann da der Wir_thin zu wünschen wohl sein?
f
Stosst an, dass die Re_ben
stets reich und gut gedeihn; dann soll's Wein auch ge_ben Euch zu er_freu'n!

poco rallent.
N
Dass sie stets gut ge-deih'n! Dann schenk' den be-sten Wein ich
Chor.
Stosst an, dass die Re-ben stets reich und gut ge-deih'n!
poco rallent.
a tempo.
stets mei-nen Gä-sten ein! Den Wunsch heg' ich für Euch und auch für mich zu-gleich! Ach
a tempo.
Più lento.
Mehr kann ich heut Euch noch nicht sa-gen,
was ins-ge-heim noch et-wa wün-sche ich; doch wird schon bald viel-leicht die
Tempo.
leggiero.
Stun-de schla-gen, heut be-halt ich's noch für mich, heut be-halt ich's noch für mich! Ja

più lento.
was noch wei - ter wünschte ich, das be - halt', das be - halt' ich noch für
p colla parte.
Scherzoso.
mich! Ja, was noch wei - ter et - wa wün - schen soll - te ich, ach das be -
cresc.
A - ha, das Wei - tre, das Wei - tre be - hält sie für sich, ja, ja, das Weit - re be -
Scherzoso.
a piacere.
halt ich noch für mich!
hält sie noch für sich!
colla parte.

Nº 2. Couplets mit Chor.

H
M
Non, mon onc - le non!
Non, mon onc - le non!
cresc
ni - ren;
Va - ter;
Wir sah'n schon das und dies, seit - dem du
Wir sah'n die Tui - le - rien, wir stürm - ten
Si, mon onc - le
Si, mon onc - le
in Pa - ris: ich liess dir in Ver - sailles die Was - ser springen.
Bat - te - rie'n von Fla - schen beim Di - ni - ren und Sou - pi - ren.
si!
si!
Ich zeigt' dir Man - cher - lei, was se - hens - wür - dig sei: Du schienest
Und um zu tan - zen flott die Gigue und die Gavott' musst ich in's
pp
Oui, mon onc - le, oui!
Oui, mon onc - le, oui!
ganz frap - pirt von man - chen Din - gen;
blau - e Zif - fer - blatt dich füh - ren.
pp

Cantabile.
H
Doch dein Ver_stand bleibt stehn, _ wenn Na_non Du ge_sehn,
Bleib jetzt be_wun_dernd stehn, _ vor die_ser Wirthin schön,
sie die so rei_zend lä_chelt
M
Comment, comment?
zum Verlie_ben:
Sie wird durch Nichts verführt, _ bleibt immer un_ge_rührt, sie
dol.
p (ungläubig)
(seufzend)
Vrai_ment? Vraiment?
(sentimental) p
ist's so_gar mir vis à vis, mir vis à vis ge_blie_ben!
Vrai_
rallent.
ppp
p (munter und leicht)
Ja dann ist
ment? _ Da_rum ist die_se Na_non heut die grösste Se_henswür_dig_keit!
f
a tempo.
pp
p

H
die-se Na-non heut die grös-ste Se-hens-wür-dig-keit die grös-ste
M
die grös-ste
Nanon.
cresc.
Beschrie-ben werd' ich wahr-lich heut, wie ei-ne Se-hens-wür-dig-
H
Se-hens-wür-dig-keit! Die grös-te Se-hens-wür-dig-
M
Se-hens-wür-dig-keit! Die grös-te Se-hens-wür-dig-
Chor.
Ja Na-non ist wohl heut die grös-te Se-hens-wür-dig-
Ja Na-non ist wohl heut die grösste Se-hens-wür-dig-
1.
2.
N
keit!
H
keit!
M
keit!
2. Ich führt' dich
keit!
accel.

Nº 3. Lied.

Allegro non troppo.
Nanon.
Hector.
Marsillac.
Piano.
Einst_mals hielt vor die_ser Schen_ke Kö_nig Lud_wig hoch zu Ross: „He, schafft
Seit dies Fac_tum hier pas_si_ret, kam die Schen_ke sehr in Flor; Je_der
ir_gend ein Ge_trän_ke; un_ser Durst ist rie_sen_gross! Schnell aus des
lobt, wie sich's ge_büh_ret, was man ihm auch se_tze vor. Die Ho_hen
Kel_ler's be_stem Fas_se ward ihm ein Glas Bordeaux ge_reicht; mit ei_ner
Herr_en, sie be_ehr_ten die_ses be_scheid_ne Haus fort_an; ne_ben dem
zwei_feln_den Gri_mas_se sah er sich's an und seufz_te leicht.
Wein sie wohl be_gehr_ten man_cher_lei An dres dann und wann.

Doch da der Trunk ihm wohl be_hag_te, an_dert die Mie_ne er to_
Solch ei_nen Ge_ckenes auch be_hag_te, füllt ich mit Krä_tzer den Po_
tal, schnalzt mit der Zun ge: (schnalzt) und sag_te: Gleich pro_birn wir's noch ein_
kal, schnalzt mit der Zung' er, und sag_te: Ach pro_birn wir's noch ein_
mal! Mmm (schnalzt) in der That, (schnalzt) in der That (schnalzt) de_li_cat. (schnalzt) Mmm
mal! Mmm in der That, Mmm de_li_cat. Mmm
Ven_tre saint gris; Ven_tre saint gris, der ist an_ge_nehm, der ist
Ven_tre saint gris; Ven_tre saint gris, schmeckts auch säu_er_lich, schmeckts auch
an_ge_nehm! Reicht mir noch ein Glas von dem ja noch ein Glas von
säu_er_lich, Nec_tar wird der Trank durch dich, ja Nec_tar wird's durch
cresc.

N
H
M
dem! Ven_tre saint gris, ❄ ven_tre saint gris der ist an_ge_nehm, der ist
dich! schmeckts auch säu_er_lich, schmeckts auch
Ven_tre saint gris, ❄ ven_tre saint gris der ist an_ge_nehm, der ist
schmeckts auch säu_er_lich, schmeckts auch
Ven_tre saint gris, ❄ ven_tre saint gris der ist an_ge_nehm, der ist
schmeckts auch säu_er_lich, schmeckts auch
an_ge_nehm, reicht mir noch ein Glas von dem, noch ein Glas von
säu_er_lich, Nec_tar wird der Trank durch dich, Nec_tar wird's durch
an_ge_nehm, reicht mir noch ein Glas von dem, noch ein Glas von
säu_er_lich, Nec_tar wird der Trank durch dich, Nec_tar wird's durch
an_ge_nehm, reicht mir noch ein Glas von dem, noch ein Glas von
säu_er_lich, Nec_tar wird der Trank durch dich, ja Nec_tar wird's durch
dem!
dich!
dem!
dich!
dem!
dich!
(❄ Durch die Note ist das Zungenschnalzen angedeutet)

Nº 4. Aufmarsch der Trommler und Pfeifer und Minnelied.

Minnelied. Allegretto non troppo.
f
p
d'Aubigné.
Was ist denn heut wohl für ein Tag, dass mir so froh zu Sinn?
Laut kün_det mir des Her_zens Schlag, dass heut ich see_lig bin!
Ei, heut ist An_na, Sanct An_na, Sanct An_na!
rall.
Kein schön_rer Tag noch war im gan_zen lie_ben lan_gen Jahr!

a tempo
An_na, zu Dir ist mein lieb_ster Gang, mein lieb_ster Gang, mein
pp
lieb_ster Gang! An_na, Dir tö_net mein be_ster Sang, mein be_ster Sang, mein
rall.
a tempo
be_ster Sang! An_na, An_nett_chen, welch' hol_der Klang, welch' hol_der Klang, welch'
pp
f
f rall.
hol_der Klang! An_na, Dir sing' ich mein Le_belang! Ja, mein Le_be_lang!

Nº5. Duett.

Allegretto.
Nanon.
Ninon.
Piano.
Setzen den Fall wir
nur, dass Sie an Ni_nons Stel_le wä_ren:
Was wür_de Na_non thun um sich
L'istesso tempo.
de_rer, die sie ver_eh_ren, die nach ihr seuf_zend schmachten, nach Ge_gen_
dol.
lie_be trachten, sich Al_ler de_rer zu er_weh_ren?
Nanon.
O ich
wüss_te schon, was ich thu!
Hö_ren Sie zu:
Da wär' ich be_gie_rig.
Meno.

Nanon (frei declamirt.)
Wenn ich je_mals soll_te spü_ren, dass ein Mann, mich könnt' ver_führen, dass sein
Wenn mir Ei_ner schien ge_fährlich und ich wüsst, er meint's nicht ehrlich, blieb' in
Wä_re Al_les Dies ver_ge_bens würd' an Stel_le stillen Er_gebens in dem
p
rall.
mf
pp
Blick mein Herz könnt' rüh_ren, säh' ich sol_chen hüb_schen Mann ein_fach
sei_ner Näh' ich schwerlich, käm' ihm gar nicht in's Ge_beg, ging' ihm
Klo_ster ich zeit_le_bens schwö_ren ab der Lie_be Freud, nähm' ein
rall.
dol.
a tempo.
lie_ber gar nicht an!
gänzlich aus dem Weg!
schwarzes Non_nen_kleid!
mit vollen Ton.
dol.
Die Män_ner gar nicht an zu sehn,
Den Männern aus dem Weg zu gehn,
Der Lieb' ent_sa_gen, in's Kloster gehn,
dazu wird Ninon sich nie ver_
a tempo.
pp
un poco acceler.
p
rall.
ff
Nie? Nie? Ni_non nie? Non!
(leicht)
ff
stehn! Non! Non! Ni_non nie? Non!
rall.
f

Più moto.
Frei_lich ist Ni_nons Schönheit so gross, dass ihr Je_der_mañ muss huldgen, drum ist sie
p
leich_ter zu ent_schuldgen. Manches ist auch Verläumdung blos. Die bö_sen Zun_gen am Hof nicht
Ninon.
rit.
a tempo.
ruhn. Ich möcht' ihr ja nicht Un_recht thun; die Liebha_ber zähl' an den Fingern ich
Nanon.
(lustig.)
her.
(mit Humor, darauf eingehend.)
Gut, doch ich bit_te, sich nicht zu ver_zäh_len.
(eifrig.)
Ein Dutzend ist's si_cher, vielleicht auch noch
mehr.
(ironisch.)
Vielleicht, dass doch Ein'_ge noch da_ran feh_len!
ff
sf

Allegretto.
Un poco moderato. (an den Fingern zählend.)
Da ist erst Vil-lar-ceau, der schö-ne Ver-se schreibt.
Ach
sf p rallent.
p
Ver-se sind's die Frauen stets be-ha-gen.
Nummro Eins! Con-dè, der Held, der im-mer Sieger bleibt,
den
sf
p
Hel-den konn-te Ni-non auch nicht schla-gen!
Nummro Zwei! Dann Au-bi-gnè, der
sf
p
zar-te Lie-der singt.
Mit ei-ner Stim-me, die zum Her-zen dringt!
Nummro Drei!

Lau_zun, der vir_tu_os die Har_fe spielt.
Nummro Vier!
Wo ist das Weib, das bei Musik nicht fühlt?
Se_vi_gnè
De Mail_ly.
La
sitzt zu Pferd, so e_le_gant.
Als Tän_zer sehr ge_wandt.
Châ_tre dann!
Wie viel
Hal_ten Sie ein! Soll_ten das ge_nug nicht schon sein?
ha_ben wir? Ich glau_be Acht!
Nein Acht, Nein Acht!
Ich glau_be Sieb'n, Nein Sieb'n, Das kann nicht
acceler.
cresc.
fp Ruhiger.

sein; wa_rum nicht gar Neun? Re_ca_pi_tu_li_ren wir, wie viel's zu_sam_men
p
decresc.
Animato.
Ja zäh_len wir!
Villarceau,
macht. A_ber ge_ben Sie hübsch Acht!
Eins,
pp
Con_dè dann Hen_ri d'Au_bi_gnè
Lau_zun,
Zwei!
Macht Drei!
Vier,
mf
p
p
Se_vi_gnè, de Mail_ly la Châ_tre.
Fünf
Sechs
Sieb'n! Bei die_sem sind wir
mf

Nun kä_me Crè_qui, Acht, Con_ti, Neun!
stehn ge_blie_ben!
Jetzt dürf_ten wir zu
p
fz
Ne_vers und Bou_flers sind ver_ges_sen.
Ganz
En_de sein.
Das wä_ren Elf.
fz
p stacc.
poco rit.
recht! In_des_sen, wenn man den Leu_ten glauben soll, so wär' be_reits das Dutzend voll.
O
poco rit.
a tempo.
ha ha ha ha ha ha ha!
Nein, da macht man's gar zu toll, ha ha ha ha ha!
a tempo.

Allegretto mosso.
Eins, Zwei, Drei, Vier, Fünf, Sechs, Siebn, Acht, Neun, Zehn, Elf sind wohl_ge_zählt.
Eins, Zwei, Drei, Vier, Fünf, Sechs, Siebn, Acht, Neun, Zehn, Elf sind wohl_ge_zählt.
Scha_de, dass noch Ei_ner fehlt, ein Dutzend wär's dann grad! Wie schad! Doch die_se Hi_
Scha_de, dass noch Ei_ner fehlt, ein Dutzend wär's dann grad! Wie schad! Doch die_se Hi_
stör_chen sind oft wohl nur Mär_chen, sie liebt Un_ter_hal_tung und Scherz. Und ist's auch nicht
stör_chen sind oft wohl nur Mär_chen, sie liebt Un_ter_hal_tung und Scherz. Und ist's auch nicht
Sit_te, was will man, ich bit_te, sie hat ein em_pfind_sa_mes Herz.
Sit_te, was will man, ich bit_te, sie hat ein em_pfind_sa_mes Herz. Dass
Nanon.
man sie um_rin_get, sie fei_ert, be_sin_get, viel Fein_de und Nei_der ihr schuf; das

muss man be_den_ken und Nachsicht ihr schenken; sie ist so schlimm nicht als ihr Ruf, __
Vivace.
crese.
pp
sie ist wohl bes_ser als ihr Ruf, sie ist so schlimm nicht als ihr Ruf, ha ha ha ha ha ha, so
sie ist wohl bes_ser als ihr Ruf, sie ist so schlimm nicht als ihr Ruf, ha ha ha ha ha ha, so
schlim, so schlim nicht als ihr Ruf, sie ist weit bes_ser als ihr Ruf, sie ist so schlim nicht als ihr
schlim, so schlim nicht als ihr Ruf, sie ist weit bes_ser als ihr Ruf, sie ist so schlim nicht als ihr
Ruf; ha ha ha ha ha ha so schlim, so schlim nicht als ihr Ruf!
Ruf; ha ha ha ha ha ha so schlim, so schlim nicht als ihr Ruf!

Nº6. Quartett.

(auf Nanon zu taumelnd.)
H
de (schnalzt) de_li_cat! (schnalzend) de de de_li_cat, Mmm
M
de (schnalzt) de_li_cat! (schnalzend) de de de_li_cat, Mmm
p
Nanon (ihnen ausweichend.)
Ventre Saint_gris, das wird un_an_ge_nehm!
Allegro.
H
ff
Na_non, noch ein Glas von dem! Der
M
ff
Na_non, noch ein Glas von dem!
ff
tr
p
(ausweichend)
N
Gebt frei mir die Pas_
H
Wein gab mir Cou_ra_ge, jetzt fühl' ich mich als Mann!
tr
sa_ge!
Lasst
Na_non! Ein Küsschen mir!
Schau nur den Schlin_gel an! Ha, ha, ha, ha,
tr
f
f

Aubignè (tritt plötzlich dazwischen)
N
ab! Hin_weg von mir! Lasst ab! Hin_weg! Ha
H
Zu mir! Zu mir! Hab' ich
M
ha ha ha ha! So fang sie dir! Ha ha! Hab' ich
N
Aubignè.
Grignan! Jetzt gehts nicht gut!
Him_mel Donner wetter noch ein_mal!
H
dich! (Mars. und Hect. halten sich gegenseitig umschlungen)
(seinen Neffen erkenend)
M
dich!
Hab' ich dich!
(für sich) (tritt schnell auf die andere Seite u. verbirgt sein Gesicht im Taschentuch)
A
Mar_sillac! Fa_tal!
(seinen Onkel erkennend)
H
Dich hab ich?

Moderato.
Nanon. p
Marsillac.
Hector.
Mein
O_ho! Wer ist deñ der? Mit wem hab' ich die Ehr?
pp
N
Bräu_ti_gam ist er; geh'n Sie ihm aus dem We_ge sonst setzt es si_cher Schlä_ge.
Aubigné.
Mar_sil_lac, E_le_ment! Dass der mich nicht er_kennt.
Hector.
Es setzt? Wie
Marsillac.
A_ha! So_so! Wie
sf
pp
pp
N
Geh'n Sie ihm aus dem We_ge, sonst setzt es si_cher Schlä_ge.
p
A
Wenn man mich hier erkennt, ist mein Ro_man zu End!
H
so? Wie Schlä_ge? Sapperment!
M
Schlä_ge? Sapperment!

(sehr sanft)
N
Grig - nan, mein Freund,
A
Wenn man mich hier er-
H
Das wär' in - per - ti - nent!
M
Das wär' in - per - ti - nent,
dol.
N
mä - ssi - ge dich! Bleib hübsch ru - hig, denk' an
A
kennt, wär' mein Roman zu End!
p
H
Drum ru - hig,
Wie Schlä - ge? Wie
p
M
Wie Schlä - ge? Wie
N
mich! Wenn du mich liebst, blei - be ru - hig steh'n! Wenn du mich liebst, lass die Nar - ren
rall.
A
Nur ru - hig! Man darf mich ja nicht
rall.
H
Schlä - ge? Das wär schön; das wär schön; das wär
rall.
M
Schlä - ge? Das wär schön; das wär schön; das wär
rall.
pp
rall.

Moderato, quasi Recitativ.
N
gehn!
Ach ja, kommen Sie ihm nicht zu nah, bringen Sie ihn nicht in
A
sehn!
H
schön!
a piacere.
M
schön!
Al_so, dein Bräutigam?
p
N
Wuth, ein Lö_we ist's an Wuth.
(für sich.)
A
Könnt' ich mich rä_chen, dürft ich mich zei_gen, müsst ich nicht
H
Ein Lö_we?
M
Ein
pp
N
Ja!
A
schweigen, gern würd' ich Beiden die Knochen zerbrechen! (Dumpf knirschend, gleichsam brül_lend.)
Im
H
Die
M
Lö_we?
Die
* Bei der Aufführung werden die Tacte bis zum * auf pag. 46 gestrichen.
p
ff
f

Allegretto un poco moderato. p
N
A
H
M
Lö_we ist's an Muth; dies dum_pfe, inn'_re Knurren, dies un_heil_vol_le
Fie_ber wallt mein Blut; ich wag es kaum zu murren, nur lei_se darf ich
Lö_we ist's an Muth; Ja, ja, ich hör' ihn knurren, das un_heil_vol_le
Lö_we ist's an Muth; Ja, ja, ich hör' ihn knurren, das un_heil_vol_le
Mur_ren, das Knur_ren, das Mur_ren, ver_kün_det sei_ne Wuth!
knur_ren, nur Knur_ren, nur Mur_ren, kaum zähm ich mei_ne Wuth!
Mur_ren, das Knur_ren, das Mur_ren, kaum zähm ich mei_ne Wuth!
Mur_ren, das Knur_ren, das Mur_ren, kaum zähm ich mei_ne Wuth!
Sie wer_den sehn, Sie wer_den sehn, Sie wer_den sehn, das en_det
wenn sie nicht gehn, so en_dets
Wir wol_len gehn, Wir wol_len gehn, Wir wol_len gehn, sonst endets
Wir wol_len gehn, Wir wol_len gehn, Wir wol_len gehn, sonst endets

Più mosso
N
A
H
M
nim - mer gut! Sein Grimm ist schon wach und bald rächt er die Schmach, doch der
nim - mer gut! Mein Grimm ist schon wach und bald räch' ich die Schmach, doch der
nim - mer gut! Sein Grimm ist schon wach und er rächt wohl die Schmach, doch der
nim - mer gut! Sein Grimm ist schon wach und er rächt wohl die Schmach, doch der
Klüg - ste, der Klüg - ste, der Klüg - ste giebt nach! Sein Grimm ist schon wach und bald
Klüg - ste, der Klüg - ste, der Klüg - ste giebt nach! Mein Grimm ist schon wach und bald
Klüg - ste, der Klüg - ste, der Klüg - ste giebt nach! Sein Grimm ist schon wach und er
Klüg - ste, der Klüg - ste, der Klüg - ste giebt nach! Sein Grimm ist schon wach und er
rächt er die Schmach, doch der Klügste, der Klügste, der Klügste, der Klügste giebt nach!
räch' ich die Schmach, doch der Klügste, der Klügste, der Klügste, der Klügste giebt nach!
rächt wohl die Schmach, doch der Klügste, der Klügste, der Klügste, der Klügste giebt nach!
rächt wohl die Schmach, doch der Klügste, der Klügste, der Klügste, der Klügste giebt nach!

Un poco meno.
Marsillac.
Das wär' ein Lö_we? Wirk_lich? Ei!
p
Hector
Beisst er?
M
Nein, der wird schwer_lich beis_sen; Muss Zahn_weh ha_ben, der
M
grim_me Leu; Kö_nig der Wü_ste, lass ihn reis_sen, lass ihn reis_sen!
(grimmig knirschend vor Zorn)
Hector. (Aubignè mit dem Finger reizend)
A
Ks, ks, bra_vo!
(schlägt Aubignè auf die Schulter)
Horch wie hübsch er kann brül_len!
sf
p
f
Nanon.
Nur nicht ihn reizen, um des Him_mels Wil_len!
H
gut gebrüllt!
Ks, ks!
Marsillac.
Ks, ks!

N
H
M
Wenn er an_fängt, ist er fürchterlich!
O der scheint nicht gar so wild!
Aber er fängt gar nicht
A
Lassen Sie endlich uns al_lein!
Kaum halt ich mich!
an!
's muss ein ge_zähmter Lö_we sein!
rit.
Tempo I.
Sein
Mein
Sein
Sein
Grimm ist schon wach und bald rächt er die Schmach, doch der Klügste, der Klügste, der Klügste giebt
Grimm ist schon wach und bald räch' ich die Schmach, doch der Klügste, der Klügste, der Klügste giebt
Grimm ist schon wach und er rächt wohl die Schmach, doch der Klügste, der Klügste, der Klügste giebt
Grimm ist schon wach und er rächt wohl die Schmach, doch der Klügste, der Klügste, der Klügste giebt

N
A
H
M
nach! Sein Grimm ist schon wach und bald rächt er die Schmach, doch der Klügste, der Klügste, der Klügste, der
nach! Mein Grimm ist schon wach und bald räch' ich die Schmach, doch der Klügste, der Klügste, der Klügste, der
nach! Sein Grimm ist schon wach und er rächt wohl die Schmach, doch der Klügste, der Klügste, der Klügste, der
nach! Sein Grimm ist schon wach und er rächt wohl die Schmach, doch der Klügste, der Klügste, der Klügste, der
Un poco meno mosso.
Klügste giebt nach!
Klügste giebt nach!
Klüg_ste giebt nach!
Klüg_ste giebt nach!
(im Abgehen)
Ks!
(im Abgehen)
Allegro.
Ks!

Nº 7. Finale I.

Allegretto un poco moderato.
mf
cresc.
f
Pierre singt in dem ganzen Finale alle Chorstellen Ten II. mit.
Chor.
Sop.
Hier sind al - le An - ver - wand - ten, Vet - tern, Ba - sen
Ten.
Bass.
fz
On - kel, Tan - ten, die Be - kann - ten, Al - le kom - men wohl - ge - zählt, nicht Ei - ner fehlt!

Na_non lud uns ein so e_ben, will ein gros_ses Fest uns ge_ben, sie soll
le_ben! Je_der hat mit Vor_be_dacht' was mit ge_bracht! Na_non, Je_der steht be_reit,
Dich zu ü_ber_raschen heut; bringt dir man_che Klei_nig_keit und wir hof_fen

dass dichs freut! Wir hoffen,dass dichs freut, wir hoffen,dass dichs freut! Sieh hier Al_le
Wir hof_fen dass dichs freut, wir hof_fen es!
An_ver_wandten, Vettern, Ba_sen, On_kel, Tanten, die Be_kannten, Al_le kom_men wohl_ge_
zählt, nicht Einer fehlt. Na_non lud uns ein so e_ben, will ein grosses Fest hier geben, sie soll

le.ben, Je.der hat mit Vor.be.dacht' was mit.gebracht; wir hof.fen dass dies
freut, wir hof.fen, dass dich's freut!
Pierre.
Schau, Onkel Mathieu bringt ein Schweinchen, u. solch'ein Schweinchen bringt dir Glück. Hier Pa.pa
Bertrand bringt ein Weinchen, das bringet auch kein Missge.schick! Mut.ter Li.set.te bringt die

rall.
Mit Gefühl.
rall.
Butter, wie man sie kaum noch keñet hier; sie gab der Kuh das beste Fut_ter, die gab die be_ste
Milch da_für! Sie gab der Kuh das be_ste Fut_ter, die gab ihr beste Milch da_für!
Sie gab der Kuh das be_ste Fut_ter, die gab ihr beste Milch da_für!
Chor.
tr
f
p
Schau hier die di_cke Tan_te The_re_se, ihr macht' der
Weg gar schwere Müh; sie bringt dir ein Paar Rie_sen_kä_se, die noch viel fet_ter sind als
sie. Vet_ter Je_rô_me bringt Speck und Schinken, Jean ist mit zwei Paar Hühnern da!

espress.
Ma - ri - on end - lich bringt sich sel - ber, denn sie ist selbst ein Gan - serl
tr
ja! Ma - ri - on end - lich bringt sich sel - ber, denn sie ist selbst ein Ganserl ja!
Ma - ri - on end - lich bringt sich sel - ber, denn sie ist selbst ein Ganserl ja!
tr
Schneller.
Ha ha ha ha ha ha ha ha ha ha ha ha ha ha ha ha! Sieh hier Al - le
Tempo I.
An - ver - wandten, Vet - ter, Ba - sen, On - kel, Tanten, die Be - kannten, al - le kom - men wohlge -

zählt, nicht Ei_ner fehlt. Na_non lud uns ein so e_ben, will ein gro_sses
Fest hier ge_ben, sie soll le_ben; Je_der hat mit Vor_be_dacht, was mit_ge_bracht, wir hof_fen
dass dich's freut, wir hof_fen, dass dich's freut!

Pierre (zu Nanon)
Ja wir sind Al_le da, die du heut her_be_stellt;
Allegretto.
Nanon.
Hier steht mein Bräu_ti_gam; sagt wie der Euch gefällt.
(Aubigné für sich)
Mir scheint, ich mach' Ef_fect!
Chor.
Der ist schön, ich muss ge_stehn!
Pierre.
Al_le Wet_ter, solch ein Vetter weckt in mir Re_spect!
Ein wahrer Prachtsoldat! in der That, in der That.
Die_ser Herr von Mi_li_tär

P
kommt mir sehr in die Quer! Ha! Potz Blitz! Das war ein Witz! Ich

Potz Blitz, das war ein gu_ter Witz.

(sich Aubigné vorstellend)

P
bin der Vet_ter Pierre genannt, als grösster Witzbold rings bekannt, reiss Wi_tze, dass es

Aubigné (bei Seite)
Mein Vetter, der! O, wie char_mant!

P
schon 'ne Schand, drum neu_er Vet_ter Eu_re Hand.

Chor
Sopr. Alt.
Horch, zu dem Bun_de naht schon die Stun_de, ein_mal schlug die Glo_cke schon!

Ten.

Bass.

Aubigne (für sich)
Wel_che Si _ tua_tion; Und Bom_bar_di_ni zö_gert noch!
Più mosso.
Pierre
Ei, was ist das? Schaut dorthin doch,schaut dorthin doch!
mf
acceler.
f
Allegro
f
Die Trommler u. Pfeifer.
Chor Sopr u. Alt
Jetzt ha_ben wir ge_trun_ken, wir sassen lang beim Wein! Jetzt
p
p
woll'n wir auch tan _ zen, bei Al_lem woll'n wir sein! Die Trommeln und die
Pfei _ fen lasst bei den Flaschen ruhn! Hol_la, Ihr Mu_si_kan_ten, zum Tan_ze spielt uns

nun!
Chor.
Hol - la, Ihr Mu - si - kanten, hol - la, Ihr Mu - si - kanten, zum Tan - ze spielt uns
nun, zum Tanz, zum Tanz!
(Allgemeiner Tanz)
Nanon.
Der No -

Aubigné (für sich)
N
tar!
Jetzt wird es Ernst für-
Chor.
Der No-tar! Jetzt wird es Ernst für-wahr!
mf
Nanon.
A
wahr!
Jetzt wird es Ernst, schon harrt der No-tar! —
pp
Aubigné (für sich.)
Soll ich ihr die Wahrheit sa-gen? Würde die Schmach sie er-tra-gen? Län-ger darf ich
täuschen sie nicht, muss fliehen, ob das Herz auch bricht!
Glocke
p

Horch zu dem Bun - de naht schon die Stun - de, zwei - mal tönt die Glo - cke schon.
Aubigné (für sich)
Wel - che Si - tua - tion, und Bombar - di - ni zö - gert noch!
Nanon.
Grignan mein Freund! so komme doch!
Moderato.
Nanon schreibt u. spricht dabei: Nanon Patin, Schenkwirthin zum goldenen Lamm.
Nun du!
Aubigné (zögernd, für sich) Was thun?
Bombardini (leise) Sie kommen schon!
Aubigné Endlich!
Chor.
Doch höret dort!

Pierre.
Nanon.
Es nahn Sol_da_ten!
Viel_leicht noch Kame_ra_den, die
N
bei der Hochzeit wollen sein!
Corporal.
f
Was giebt es hier?
Hal_tet
Chor.
Ei_ne Hochzeit!
mf
C
ein!
Nanon col Sopr.
O_ho!
Wa_rum?
p
Was soll das sein?
p
Der Tambour Grig_nan, der sich duellirt,
f
C
wird ins Gefängniss auf der Stell' geführt!
Animato.
Nanon.
Wie? Duellirt?
Aubigne.
Ja das ist wahr!
fz

N
Und ar_re_tirt. Warum nicht gar? Er ist mein Bräutigam!
Corporal
Das ist mir ei_ner_lei, ich folge dem Be_
f
C
(Bärbeissig.)
fehl, drum kei_ne Re_de_rei! Was ein_mal comman_di_ret, das wird voll_füh_ret;
wir fol_gen unsrer Pflicht und muk_sen nicht! Was einmal comman_di_ret, das wird vollführet;
(Den Corporal nachahmend.)
Chor.
Was einmal comman_di_ret, das wird vollführet;
mf
wir folgen streng der Pflicht und muksen nicht! Wir muk_sen nicht!
Nanon
Wie, Ihr
sie folgen streng der Pflicht und muksen nicht! Sie muk_sen nicht!
Sie muk_sen nicht!
Agitato.
pp

N
woll_tet ihn — mir rau_ben, nein, — ach ich kañ es nicht glauben, s'ist nicht möglich, kañ nicht
fs
N
sein! Ich kañ's nicht glauben! Es darf nicht
Aubigné.
Ach ihr Schmerz zerreisst mein Herz! Ach ihr Schmerz zerreisst mein
Corporal.
Da hilft kein Weinen und kein Schrei'n! Es muß ja sein!
Fort nur
cresc.
N
sein! Nein! —
Andante.
A
(f.s.)
Herz! Ach ihr Schmerz — zerreisst mein Herz! Ach das
C
Fort nur fort, nur fort, nur fort, es muß ja sein! —
Ar_me Na_non er_gieb — dich drein!
fort! Nur fort, nur fort, es muß ja sein!
Andante.
ff
p
p

A
Spiel, das ich ge_trie_ben, bit_ter rächt_ es jetzt sich hier! Sie nur werd' ich e_wig
Nanon.
Nur ein Traum_bild ist ge_
dol.
lie_ben, und mein Herz_ es bleibt bei ihr,_ ja mein Herz_ es bleibt bei
mf
p
pp
N
blie_ben, was so hold_ ge_lä_chelt mir! All mein Glück_ war nur sein
ihr! ich fühl es hier, ich fühl_ es
C
Sie wird e_wig ihn
dol.
Lie_ben all mein Glück war sein Lie_ben, mein Glück war sein Lie_ben und ihr
hier! Sie war e_wig ich lie_ben, ja e_wig ich lie_ben!
lie_ben, a_ber er muss fort er muss fort, er muss fort, er muss fort!
Chor.
pp
Sie wird ihn e_wig e_wig lie_ben,

rallent.
Più lento.
raubt, ach Ihr raubt ihn grau - sam mir! Ach Ihr
denn mein Herz ach mein Herz bleibt bei ihr!
ja wir füh - ren fort ihn von hier. ja wir füh-ren ihn
ach sie wird ihn e-wig lie-ben, e - wig und man
wird ihn e - wig lie - ben!
kön-tet jetzt grausam ihn rau-ben mir!
Ach mein Herz, mein Herz bleibt hier!
fort, von hier, er muss fort von hier!
rei - sset grausam ihn jetzt von ihr!
und man reisst ihn von ihr!
reisst ihn grausam von ihr!

Allegro non troppo.
Nanon (zusammensinkend.)
Weh' mir!
Aubigné (indem er fortgeführt wird.)
Na_non, leb wohl, leb_ wohl!
Più mosso.
trem.
Allegro.
Chor.
Arretirt, condemnirt, in Arrest fortgeführt;
ihm droht der Tod, weil er sich du_el_lirt, du_el_lirt! Ar_re_tirt, condemnirt,

Nanon.
Ach – ihn
in Arrest fort_geführt, am Hochzeits_ta_ge ist das pas_sirt!
lieb' ich mehr als mein Le_ben; wird er nicht zu_rück mir ge_ge_ben,
kann mir Nichts mehr Trost ver_leihn, wer wird ihm ein Retter sein!
Ach ihn lieb ich mehr als mein Le_ben, wird er nicht zu_rück mir ge_ge_ben
Wer kann ih_ren Muth neu be_le_ben? Den Ver_lor_nen wie_der ihr ge_ben!

rall.
kann mir Nichts mehr Trost ver_leihn, wer wird Ret_ter ihm sein!
Wer kann der Ar_men Trost ver_leihn, wer wird Ret_ter ihm sein!
a tempo.
fz
rall.
Allegretto.
Gaston.
Mich sen_det
p
pp
G
mei_ne schö_ne Her_rin her zu Eu_rem Eh_ren_tag, mit die_sem
Rin_ge hier, doch was ist das? Die Au_gen Thränenschwer. Was
fehlt der schönen Braut? Der Bräutgam feh_let mir!
Nanon.
Doch

N
accelerat.
Ihr bringt neu-en Hoff-nungs-schim-mer: Ni-non wird hel-fen, sie hilft ja
accelerat.
Gaston.
im-mer, nicht wahr? Ge-wiss! Sie hilft, wo sie kann;
cresc.
doch was ist's mit dem Bräuti-gam, sagt an? Arretirt, condemmnirt,
Nanon.
in Arrest fort-ge-führt; ihm droht der Tod, weil er sich du-el-lirt! Duel-lirt?
Gaston.
G
Arre-tirt, condemmnirt, in Arrest fort-geführt, am Hochzeitsta-ge ist das pas-sirt!
Chor.
Arre-tirt, condemmnirt, in Arrest fort-geführt, am Hochzeitsta-ge ist das pas-sirt!

N
Ni - non soll ihn wie-der mir ge - ben, den ich lie - be mehr als mein
G
Ni - non soll ihn wie-der dir ge - ben, den du lie - best mehr als dein
p
N
Le - ben! Sie wird mir ih - ren Bei - stand leih'n, sie wird Retterin uns sein,
G
Le - ben! Sie wird Dir ih - ren Bei - stand leih'n, sie wird Retterin uns sein,
p
N
Ja
G
Ja
Chor.
Ni - non soll zu - rück ihn dir ge - ben denn du lieb - test mehr als dein
mf

N
G
rit.
Sie wird uns ih - ren Bei - stand leihn, wird uns Ret - te - rin
Sie wird uns ih - ren Bei - stand leihn, wird uns Ret - te - rin
Le - ben, Sie wird Euch ih - ren Bei - stand leihn, wird Euch Ret - te - rin
fz
Allegro.
p
cresc.
sein! Ja Ni - non, sie vermags al - lein, ver - mags al - lein! Ja, Ni - non
sein! Ja Ni - non, sie vermags al - lein, ver - mags al - lein! Ja, Ni - non
sein! Ja Ni - non, sie vermags al - lein, ver - mags al - lein! Ja, Ni - non

sie vermags al. lein vermags al. lein, ja
sie vermags al. lein vermags al. lein, ja
sie vermags al. lein vermags al. lein, ja Ni. non wird Euch
al. lein!
al. lein!
Bei. stand leihn!

II. ACT.

Nº 8. Entre-Act und Chor.

Vorhang auf.

mf

cresc.

ff

Chor.

Sopr. *f*

Bei Ni-non sich ein-zu-füh-ren im Sa-lon zu pro-me-

Ten. *f*

Bass. *f*

Im Sa-lon zu pro-me-

ff

tr

ni-ren gilt Al-len als ho-he Gunst. Hier hört man ge-pries'ne Hel-den und er-

tr

lauch - te Na_men mel_den nebst He_ro_en der Kunst! Ja bei
und er_lauch_te Na_men
tr
mf
Ni non de l'Lenclos ge_nie_sset man die Stun_den froh! Ja bei
Ni_non de l'En_clos ge_nie_sset man die Stun_den froh!
cresc.

Nº 8½. (Wurde bei der Aufführung fortgelassen)

G
Schö - ne Frau - en, die Ihr wollt e - wig blei - ben jung und hold,
Wollt Ihr Herrn, durch Con - ver - sir'n glän - zen, blen - den und ver - führ'n,
lento.
a tempo.
blei - bet à la Ni - non!
re - det à la Ni - non!
pp
rall.
Die Coif - fü - re, die Euch schmückt, Al - les durch Ge - schmack ent - zückt die ist à la
Wer den Ar - men ger - ne giebt, Wohlthun oh - ne Prun - ken liebt, der giebt à la
Ni - non!
Ni - non!
1.
2.
Meno
mosso.
Meno mosso.
Mit dem Him - mel gut zu stehn, und Ge - bet er - hört zu sehn,

Tempo I
be - tet à la Ni - non!
Und die
accel.
Lieb — die kur - ze Zeit stets nur blüht, doch oft sich erneut, die heisst à — la
leggiero.
Ni - non, die heisst à la Ni - non, die heisst à la Ni - non, ja die Lie - be die
Allegro.
ach sehr kur - ze Zeit nur blüht, die heisst, — die heisst, die heisst à la Ni -
non!

№ 9. Couplets.

Allegretto moderato.
Ninon.
Piano.
Treu blieb ich stets einem Prin-
Kommt ka-tzen-boshaft mir ei-ne
In Po-li-tik wie in der
zi-pe, ja stau-net nur, auch ich bin treu! Das ist ganz leicht ein-fach zu
Freun-din, ich seh ihrs an, sie freu-et sich mir in der Eil gleich mit-zu-
Lie-be ist das Prin-zip gut an-ge-bracht. Der Di-plo-mat ist stets im
ü-ben, und un-fehl-bar pro-bat da-bei! Wie man-cher Mann wollt' mir die
thei-len die neu-sten Lü-gen ü-ber mich! O wenn Sie er-füh-ren, was
Vor-theil, der es sich ganz zu ei-gen macht. Ein Staat, der lang rüs-tet und
Lie-be ver-gel-ten durch Treu-lo-sig-keit, bis-her ist's noch Keinem ge-
ge-stern die Leu-te er-zählt, fängt sie an, Ach lei-der, ich weiss schon, er-
dro-het mit No-ten, kommt sel-ten ans Ziel! Nur der, der ganz stil-le mo-

N
lun_gen, ich liess ihm da_ zu gar nicht Zeit.
widr' ich, doch glaub' ich bei_nah nicht da_ran.
bil macht, und los geht ge_win_net das Spiel.
Da_rum nur ward ich
Sie soll_ten Ih_ren
Eh noch der Nach_bar
rall.
nie be_tro_gen weil sel_ber ich es frü_her thu;
Mann be_trü_gen? Ab_scheulich wär's! Jetzt hab' ich Ruh;
giesst die Ka_nonen, da rückt er ins Feld und schlägt ihn im Nu;
Was Du nicht willst, dass Dir gesche_he,
rall.
Ninon, Gaston, Frontenac
das fü_ge vor_her An_dern zu! Was Du nicht willst, dass Dir gesche_he das fü_ge vor_her
Houlières.
Abbé.
N
G
F
vor_her Andern zu
H
A
1.2.
3.

Nº 10. Minnelied.

rall.
a tempo.
lan - gen Jahr. An - na zu Dir ist mein lieb - ster Gang, mein
a tempo.
rall.
lieb - ster Gang, mein lieb - ster Gang; An - na, dir tö - net mein be - ster Sang, mein
be - ster Sang, mein be - ster Sang! An - na, Ni - net - ta, welch hol - der Klang, welch
hol - der Klang, welch hol - der Klang! Ni - non, dir sing ich mein
f
rall.
Le - be - lang, Ja, mein Le - be - lang!
rall.
p
f

No 10a Auftrittslied.

1. Str. (geträllert.)
2. Str. (getanzt.)
rall.
Ach ja, zur Sän_ge_rin
Ach ja, zur Tän_ge_rin
hätt ich Ta_lent charmant; na_tür_lich, denn ich bin The_a_ter In_ten_dant! Na_
hätt ich Ta_lent charmant;
tür_lich, denn ich bin The_a (lachend) ha ha ha ha ha ha a_ter, The_a_ter, The_
(schmetternd.)
a_ter_in_tendant!

Nº 11. Sextett.

N
fah - ren, was zu - rück Sie hielt.
Marsillac.
Ach es pas - sirt in heut'ger Zeit so manche nicht'ge Neu - ig -
Ninon.
Ei wirklich?
Frontenac.
Ei - ne Neuigkeit?
Houlières.
Er - zählen Sie!
M
keit, die un - ser ein's in Anspruch nimmt.
Ich bin be -
Hector
(leise z. Hector.)
Ich geb Acht!
M
reit! Jetzt gieb Acht, was sie mit dem Fächer macht, wie er spielt ob sie sich getroffen fühlt.
(leise zu Ninon.)
G
Ich schloss Aubigné ein; den Schlüssel —
(laut)
N
Gieb her! Wir lauschen schon Marquis!
Mars.
So -

(für sich.)
G
S'wird Etwas Ra_res sein!
N
Wir lauschen schon Marquis! Wir lauschen schon Marquis
F
Wir lauschen schon Marquis! Wir lauschen schon Marquis
Ho
Wir lauschen schon Marquis! Wir lauschen schon Marquis
(leise zu Hect.)
M
gleich!
Jetzt gieb
cresc.
Allegretto moderato.
Acht.
Marsillac.
Ein jun_ger
pp
Edelmann, der mir be_kannt, bei Hof wie ü_ber_all sehr gern ge sehn, zu ei_ner
Hector.
Wie sie auf hor_chen
Da_me in Be_ziehung stand, die viel_genannt, voll An_muth, Geist und schön, ja sehr

Gaston.
Das scheint mir eine Fal_le.
He
Al - le!
M
geistvoll und da_bei schön! Nun muss er mit ihr brechen, weil er Hei_rathen will
(Hector anstossend, leise.)
pp Hasst du ge_sehn, den Fächer, den Fächer,
Hector. Zu_fall vielleicht!
Mars. Nur
pp
still!
Frontenac. Was wei_ter mit dem jun_gen Mann?
Marsillac. Ach die_ser Ärmste ist sehr ü_bel
dran: Statt dass er's der Ge_liebten frei ge_steh, ist er ver_zagt und meidet ih_re Näh, sucht
lie_ber Ausflucht allerlei, der Thor, schiebt Feste, Rei_sen al_te Tan_ten vor
Front. Wie?
cresc.

F
Tanten sa_gen Sie?
Hector.
Oh schau nur den Fächer an,
Marsillac.
Ja al_te Tan_ten!
pp
Houliéres.
Und wie heisst dieser Mann?
He
Den Fächer! Zu_fall vielleicht.
Marsillac.
Der Na_me kommt zu_
Ho
(auffahrend.)
Brünett?
Front. (fächelnd.)
Brünett!
Hector.
die auch?
Gaston. (f.s.)
Jetzt fächellt ein Ter_
M
letzt! Er ist brü_nett! Brü_nett!
Zu_fall vielleicht
cresc.
decresc.
p
G
zett!
Ninon.
Wär's Au_bi_gné? Ha das wär ab_scheulich.
Frontenac.
Wär's Montausier?
Ha das wär ab_scheulich.
Houliéres.
Wär's Le Regnier?
Ha das wär ab_scheulich.
cresc.
f

N
F
Ho
wär' un-ver-zeih-lich, doch mich zu fas-sen, Nichts seh'n zu las-sen,
decresc.
Etwas bewegter.
Muss ich fä-cheln und will lä-cheln als wä-re Nichts geschehn; ja zu lä-cheln
Gaston.
Wer's ver-steht, für den ver-räth das Fächer-
und zu fä-cheln das muss man gut verstehn!
Hector.
Marsillac.

G
N
F
Ho
He
M
spiel mehr als Wor-te das Gefühl. Überraschung zu veste-cken, muss der Fächer Al-les decken;
Überraschung zu veste-cken, muss der Fächer Al-les decken;
pp
poco rit.
a tempo.
sein A-gi-ren ist von nöthen, zu ca-chiren das Erröthen: Ja zu fä-cheln und zu lä-cheln
Ja wie sie fächeln, wie sie
poco rit.
a tempo.

G
als wä - re Nichts geschehn, so zu lächeln und zu fächeln das muss man gut verstehn.
N
als wä - re Nichts geschehn, so zu lächeln und zu fächeln das muss man gut verstehn.
F
als wä - re Nichts geschehn, so zu lächeln und zu fächeln das muss man gut verstehn.
Ho
als wä - re Nichts geschehn, so zu lächeln und zu fächeln das muss man gut verstehn.
He
lächeln als wä - re Nichts geschehn, wie sie lächeln wie sie fächeln jetzt hast du's gesehn,
M
lächeln als wä - re Nichts geschehn, wie sie lächeln wie sie fächeln jetzt hast du's gesehn,
Ninon.
Nun, wei - ter! Nun?
Frontenac.
Nun, wei - ter! Nun?
Houliéres.
Nun, wei - ter! Nun?
Marsillac.
Der Mann, von dem ich sprach.
M
Der Mann, von dem ich sprach, ist wie mich däucht, auch

Alle 3 in ei-
ner Linie vortretend.)
Wie, Kammerherr? Wen Er es wä-re!
Den Namen, den Namen, ich bit-te sehr!
Kam-merherr!
Hector. Marsillac.
Jetzt al-le Drei? Das ist Zu-fall vielleicht!
Marsillac.
Nun, da es so Sie intres-sirt, es ist der Her-zog von Choi-
seul.
(f.s. schadenfroh.)
a piacere.
a tempo.
Ha, das war an-ge-führt!
Wie? Der?
Ich mein-te d'Au-bi-gnè!
Ich mein-te Montausier.
Ich mein-te De Regnier.

G
Ja zu fächeln und zu lächeln als wä_re Nichts geschehn, so zu lächeln
N
Ja zu fächeln und zu lächeln als wä_re Nichts geschehn, so zu lächeln
F
Ja zu fächeln und zu lächeln als wä_re Nichts geschehn, so zu lächeln
Ho
Ja zu fächeln und zu lächeln als wä_re Nichts geschehn so zu lächeln
He
Ja! Ja zu fächeln und zu lächeln als wä_re Nichts geschehn, so zu
M
Ja! Ja zu fächeln und zu lächeln als wä_re Nichts geschehn, so zu
G
und zu fächeln das muss man gut verstehn! Doch der Fächer in Be_wegung wird oft
N
und zu fächeln das muss man gut verstehn! Doch der Fächer in Be_wegung wird oft
F
und zu fächeln das muss man gut verstehn! Doch der Fächer in Be_wegung wird oft
Ho
und zu fächeln das muss man gut verstehn! Doch der Fächer in Be_wegung wird oft
He
lächeln, und zu fächeln das muss man gut verstehn! Doch der Fächer in Be_wegung wird oft
M
lächeln, und zu fächeln das muss man gut verstehn! Doch der Fächer in Be_wegung wird oft

G
N
F
Ho
He
M
f
p
Sprecher in Er_regung, drum heisst es lächeln und fleissig fächeln, fächeln, fächeln, fächeln,
Sprecher in Er_regung, drum heisst es lächeln und fleissig fächeln, fächeln, fächeln, fächeln,
Sprecher in Er_regung, drum heisst es lächeln und fleissig fächeln, fächeln, fächeln, fächeln,
Sprecher in Er_regung, drum heisst es lächeln und fleissig fächeln, fächeln, fächeln, fächeln,
Sprecher in Er_regung, drum heisst es lächeln und fleissig fächeln, fächeln, fächeln, fächeln,
Sprecher in Er_regung, drum heisst es lächeln und fleissig fächeln, fächeln, fächeln, fächeln,
fächeln da_bei, das Lächeln und Fächeln birgt so Man_cher_lei; drum heisst es
fächeln da_bei, das Lächeln und Fächeln birgt so Man_cher_lei; drum heisst es
fächeln da_bei, das Lächeln und Fächeln birgt so Man_cher_lei; drum heisst es
fächeln da_bei, das Lächeln und Fächeln birgt so Man_cher_lei; drum heisst es
fächeln da_bei, das Lächeln und Fächeln birgt so Man_cher_lei; drum heisst es
fächeln da_bei, das Lächeln und Fächeln birgt so Man_cher_lei; drum heisst es

sf

lächeln und fleis_sig fächeln, fächeln, fächeln, fächeln, fächeln da_bei, das Lächeln und Fächeln

lächeln und fleis_sig fächeln, fächeln, fächeln, fächeln, fächeln da_bei, das Lächeln und Fächeln

lächeln und fleis_sig fächeln, fächeln, fächeln, fächeln, fächeln da_bei, das Lächeln und Fächeln

lächeln und fleis_sig fächeln, fächeln, fächeln, fächeln, fächeln da_bei, das Lächeln und Fächeln

lächeln und fleis_sig fächeln, fächeln, fächeln, fächeln, fächeln da_bei, das Lächeln und Fächeln

lächeln und fleis_sig fächeln, fächeln, fächeln, fächeln, fächeln da_bei, das Lächeln und Fächeln

fz

tr.

birgt so Man_cher_lei!

birgt so Man_cher_lei!

birgt so Man_cher_lei!

birgt so Man_cher_lei!

birgt so Man_cher_lei!

birgt so Man_cher_lei!

№ 12. Duo.

Allegretto moderato.
Nanon.
Aubigne.
Piano.
Grignan!
Nanon!
Ist's möglich?
Ist's möglich?
Er hier?
Sie hier?
Ist's Traum, ist's Wirklichkeit?
Wel_che Ver_le_gen_heit!
Con delicatezza.
Grig_nan's E_ben_bild vor mir!
Na_non ist's! Was sucht sie hier?
Sei_ne
Zü_ge sind's und auch sein Blick!
(für sich)
(laut)
Jetzt gilt es Keckheit und Ge_schick! Was setzt

99
Nanon.
A
so dich in Er_stau_nen, lie_be Klei_ne?
Auch sei_ne Stim_me!
N
Es war, ich mei_ne,_ Ver_zei_hung, ich bin ver_wirrt gar sehr,
weiss nicht mehr, ob ich noch wie vorher richtig seh' und richtig hör';
p
Ähnlichkeit hat mich be_tro_gen, wie könnte es mög_lich sonst sein! Nein, nein!
Ahn_te sie, wie sie be_tro_gen, sie würde mir nim_mer ver_zeih'n, nein, nein!
Mich hat mein Au_ge be_lo_gen ja ja es ist Täuschung al_lein!
Frisch darauf los drum ge_lo_gen denn Dreistigkeit hilft hier al_lein!
cresc.
f

Poco più.
Aubigné.
Willst end_lich du mein Kind-mir sa_gen?
Nanon.
Er_lau_ben Sie mir ein'_ge Fra_gen,
p
denn meinen Sinnen trau'ich nicht.
Aubigné. Nanon.
rit.
Recht gern! Doch täuschen Sie mich nicht.
Das ist ein
rit.
p
Tempo I.
Stuhl, nicht wahr? Und hier ein Tisch, Das ein Ka_min? Ein Spie_gel
Das ist ganz klar. Ja!
(mit dem Finger auf Aubigné deutend)
ist da_ran? Und was ist das? Ein Mann?
Das? Je nun, das ist ein Mann!
p a piacere.
Allegro.
Ein Mann, das war auch Er! Wenn er es doch vielleicht nur wär?
ffp

N
Aubigné.
Und nun sa_gen Siegeschwind, wie Sie hei_ssen, wer Sie sind? Du scheinst neu im Hau_se hier, weil
A
ich zum er_sten Mal dich seh, Drum muss ich mich nennen dir; Ich bin Marquis d'Aubi_gné!
Nanon.
Nummro Drei, Nummro Drei, ha ich ver_steh. Und ha_ben kei_nen
N
Freund o_der Bru_der Sie, der Tam_bour ist und Grig_nan sich nennt?
N
Doch sieht er Ih_nen
A
Mit ei_nen Tambour war ich nie be_freundet o_der gar ver_wandt.

N
gar so ähn_lich! Der Mund frap_pant! Nur
A
Sehr schmeichel_haft!
et_was_ et_was mehr ge_wöhnlich. Die Na_se hab ich gleicher_
Was denn?
kannt; doch ist die Sei_ne mehr ge_mein! Die Haltung auf ein Haar nur nicht so e_le_gant, so
O_ho!
Più lento.
fein! Sein Kinn ist's auch so_gar! Nur die Pe_rü_cke, nur die Pe_rü_cke verwandelt
So, so!
Più lento.
pp

N
A
ihn ihm Au-gen-bli-cke! Ja die Pe-rü-cke, ja die Pe-rü-cke verwandelt mich zu mei-nem
a tempo.
Es kann nicht sein, mich täuscht der Schein; doch wun-der-bar bleibts im-mer-dar!
Glücke! Es muss ja sein, ich bleib von Stein doch das ist gar nicht leicht für-wahr!
a tempo.
rall.
Un poco agitato.
pp
Wenn ich in sein lie-bes Au-ge seh, glaub ich stets, ich sei in sei-ner Näh,
Wenn ich in die lie-ben Au-gen seh, o mir pocht mein Herz in Lust und Weh!
Laut ihr zu zu-ru-fen, treibt es mäch-tig mich: Na-non, theure

A
Na_non, ach wie lieb ich dich!
Nanon.
Laut hin_aus zu_
N
ru _ fen treibt es mäch_tig mich: Na_non theure Grig_nan, ach wie
A
Laut ihr zu zu_ru_fen treibt es mich: Na_non theure Na_non, ach wie
N
lieb ich dich! Mein Bräu_ti_gam war
A
lieb ich dich! Und die_ser Tambour?
a piacere
a tempo poco moderato.
N
er. Ich liebt' ihn, ich liebt' ihn, ach so sehr, doch
pp
gestern, welch ein Schmerz, ach hat man ihn weg _ ge_führt! O schwei_ge
Alt (für sich)

N
A
Und zwar, weil er sich du_el_lirt.
still, mein Herz!
Wie, weg_ge_führt?
Und da_rum, höchst wahrscheinlich wird er auf_ge_hängt so_gar,
's ist grässlich, nicht
(am seinen Hals greifend)
Al_le Wet_ter.
f
p
wahr?
Sie
Lass dei_ne Trau_er en_den, Ich wer_de mich verwenden, da er so
wollh ihn retten? Ach das ist schön. Und wird er si_cher auch ge_ hängt nicht wer_den?
ähn_lich mir soll sehn

Animato
N
A
(f.s.)
Nun, dann will
Ich glaube nicht. Obwohl ganz sicher Nichts auf Er - den!
fp
ich voll Hoff - nung gehn, will bau - en auf Ihr Wort! Auf Wie - der -
rall.
Du kannst's!
p rall.
Tempo I.
pp
sehn!
Wenn ich in sein lie - bes Au - ge seh,
Wenn ich in die lie - ben Augen seh,
glaub ich stets, ich sei in sei - ner Näh.
o wie pocht mein Herz in Lust und Weh! Laut ihr zu - zu -

A
ru - fen, treibt es mäch - tig mich: Na - non, theu - re
N
Laut hi - naus zu ru - fen
A
Na - non, ach wie lieb ich dich! Laut ihr zu - zu -
N
treibt es mäch - tig mich: Grignan, theurer Grignan, ach wie lieb' wie lieb' ich
A
ru - fen treibt es mich: Na - non, theure Na - non, ach wie lieb' wie lieb' ich
N
Dich!
A
Dich!
Mosso.

№ 13. Couplets.

Grazioso.
Hector.
Piano.
Jung an
Jun - ge
Jah - ren, un - er - fah - ren, blieb von Frau - en ich weit; wollt ver.
Mäd - chen, sind oft schüch - tern, thun ver - schämt, blei - ben stumm und dann
mei - den recht be - schei - den je - de Zu - dring - lich - keit. Doch bald
sagt man die ist nüch - tern o - der gar: Ist die dumm! Fin - de
sieht man, dass so - lid man kei - ne Sie - ge ge - winnt, wenn man
dies auch gar nicht schön ich: wird das Spröd' - thun doch fad. Doch ist

schmach - tet und nicht trach - tet, dass man zu - greift ge - schwind; bin noch
äl - ter sie ein we - nig, thut's das Ge - gen - theil grad: Statt des
poco rallent.
blöd' ich und er - röth' ich wie ein Neu - ling noch heut: Ach das
Zie - rens, des Ge - nie - ren's ko - ket - tirt fest sie heut: Ja das
poco rallent.
giebt sich und das übt sich und man lernts mit der
Zeit! Ja das giebt sich und das übt sich und man lernts mit der
Zeit!
p
ff
p

№ 14. Finale II.

Tempo di Polacca.
Piano.
pp
cresc.
Bei Ni_non sich a_mü_si_ren, im Sa_lon zu pro_me_ni_ren, gilt
Im Sa_lon zu pro_me_
Al_len als ho_he Gunst! Hier hört man ge_pries_ne Hel_den und er_

Nanon
lauch - te Na_men mel_den nebst He_ro_en der Kunst! Nun,
und er_lauchte Na_men
p
N
wa_ren Sie beim Marschall Villeroy?
Houlières.
Ich war in seinem Haus;
H
Er selbst nicht da; bei der Ge_lieb_ten hiess es, wä_re
Ninon
Und wa_rum such_ten Sie ihn nicht bei der?
H
er.
Er hat Ge_lieb_te
H
ei_ne gros_se Zahl, ich wuss_te nicht bei Welcher? Wie fa_tal!
Ninon (zu der eben eintretenden Frontenac)
Und

(zu dem ein-
Louvois?
Und Ca-
Froutenac.
War lei-der nicht zu Haus, er sei bei der Ca-mar-go gra-de.
tretenden Marsillac)
mar-go?
O wie
Marsillac.
War lei-der nicht zu Haus, sie sei bei Louvois e-ben.
scha-de! Da kön-nen vor der Hand wir gar Nichts thun; an mei-ne
Gä-ste den-ken muss ich nun!
Sopr.
Ja, bei Ni-non de l'En-clos go-nie-sset
Froutenac mit Sopr. I.
Houliéres mit Sopr. II.
Ten.
La Platre
Marsillac. mit Bass.
Bass.
mf

man die Stun_den froh; ja bei Ni_non de l'En_clos ge_niesset
cresc.
man die Stun_den froh!
Moderato.
La Platre.
Ninon.
Doch Ninon selbst macht heu_te sich so rar, bleibt fern uns stets? Ver_
p
zei_hung, es ist wahr. Doch jetzt ge_hör' ich Ihnen ganz und gar; nun Mar_sil_

Marsillac.
lac, jetzt wär- es an der Zeit, wo bleibt die Ü-ber-raschung? Schon be-reit!
rall.
ich sing ein Lied zu Ninon's Namens-tag! Von mir verfasst und in Musik ge-setzt.
pp
(für sich)
Schmück ich mich auch mit frem-den Fe-dern jetzt, der Tambour Na-nons wird verzeihn!
Ninon.
Marsillac.
Ich bitt' um Platz! Wir werden ap-plaudi-ren! Das Ball-or-che-ster ruf ich jetzt her-
f
p
ein; es soll mein Lied accompag-ni-ren.
ff

Menuett.

Auftreten des Ballets.

Camargo-Menuett.

Mosso.

Marsillac.
Nach die-sem In-ter-mez-zo kommt mein neu-es Lied da-ran, mein Lied an Ni-non,
p
M
ich fang' es an.
Allegretto un poco moderato.
f
f
M
Was ist denn heut wohl für ein Tag, dass mir so froh zu Sinn?
Ninon.
Was ist denn
N
das?
Hör' ich recht? Täuscht mich mein Ohr?
Gaston.
Das kommt bekannt mir vor.
Frontenac.
Houlières.
Was ist denn das?
Marsillac.
Laut kündet mir des Herzens Schlag, dass heut ich see-lig
La Plâtre.
Ein

Ninon.
Das Lied, das Au_bi_gnè hier sang.
Gaston.
Das Lied, das Au_bi_gnè hier sang.
Das Lied, das Au_bi_gnè hier sang
F
H
M
bin. Ei heut ist
Pl
Lied_chen, das man brau_chen kann!
M
An - na, Sankt An - na, Sankt An - na!
Pl
No_ti_ren wir's sofort; gleich mor_gen bring ich's an, an ei_nen andern Ort.
N
Wer von Bei_den will uns da
G
Was mag wohl da - hin_ter ste_cken?
M
Kein schön_rer Tag noch war im gan_zen lie_ben
Pl
Das kann man brau_chen! Sehr gut!

Più mosso.
(laut.)
ne - cken? Dies Lied, es wär von Ih - nen?
lan - gen Jahr. Ganz neu von mir, zu
Ich kenn' es schon! So hö - ren Sie! Wir stimmen ein!
Wir auch! Wir stimmen ein!
Wir auch! Wir stimmen ein!
dienen! Das kann nicht sein! Das kann nicht sein!
molto cresc.
rall.
An - na zu dir ist mein lieb - ster Gang, mein lieb - ster Gang, mein lieb - ster Gang,
An - na zu dir ist mein lieb - ster Gang, mein lieb - ster Gang, mein lieb - ster Gang,
An - na zu dir ist mein lieb - ster Gang, mein lieb - ster Gang, mein lieb - ster Gang,
An - na zu dir ist mein lieb - ster Gang, lieb - ster Gang, lieb - ster
Es wird den Au - tor angst und bang!

N
G
F
H
M
An_na, dir tö_net mein be_ster Sang, mein be_ster Sang mein be_ster Sang;
An_na, dir tö_net mein be_ster Sang, mein be_ster Sang mein be_ster Sang;
An_na, dir tö_net mein be_ster Sang, mein be_ster Sang mein be_ster Sang;
(bricht ab)
An_na, dir tö_net mein
Der Teu_fel soll's ho_len!
Weil schon bekannt sein neu_er Sang.
An_na, Ni_net_ta, welch hol_der Klang, welch hol_der Klang, welch hol_der Klang!
An_na, Ni_net_ta, welch hol_der Klang, welch hol_der Klang, welch hol_der Klang!
An_na, Ni_net_ta, welch hol_der Klang, welch hol_der Klang, welch hol_der Klang!
Ver_wünsch_ter Tambour! Verwünschter Tambour!
Seht, wie dem Au_tor angst und bang!

N
G
F
H
M
rall.
Ni_non, Dir sing' ich mein Le_be_lang, ja mein Le_be_
Ni_non, Dir sing' ich mein Le_be_lang, ja mein Le_be_
Ni_non, Dir sing' ich mein Le_be_lang, ja mein Le_be_
Der Tambour hat's si_cher ge_stoh_len Der Teu_fel soll's
Seht, wie dem Au_tor schon angst und bang, ihm ist angst und
f
rall.
a tempo.
lang!
lang!
lang!
ho_len!
bang, weil schon be_kannt sein neu_er Sang!
a tempo.
rall.

Allegro non troppo.
Ninon.
Ha Marquis d'Au - bi - gnè, zur rechten Zeit!
Aubigné.
Ver - zeihung, doch
Ninon.
Hier. Herr von Mar - sil - lac hat uns er - freut, er sang uns ein
Lied, das auch Ih - nen be - kannt?
Aubigné.
Wie, mir be - kannt? Da bin ich ge - spannt.
Da
Ca - po bit - ten wir schön!
Marsillac
Ich bin be - reit!
Gaston
Frontenac
m. Sopr I.
Houlieres
m. Sopr II.
Ja, da Ca - po bit - ten wir schön, noch ei - nen Vers!
La Plâtre m. Bass.

(f. s.)
M
Hm, hm! Mich kratzt mein Ge-wis-sen! hm! hm! Wo mein Nef-fe nur steckt? Hm!
Nanon
Ninon.
Ach, da sind Sie ja! Wie? Nanon? Sprich, was geschah?
Chor und Soli
Doch, was giebt's? Was ist ge-schehn?
cresc.
Più mosso.
Nanon.
Ni
Sprich, was ge-schah? Ach, während man hier sich a-müsirt, ist draussen ein grosses Mal
Sprich, was ge-schah?
Chor und Soli.
Più mosso.
Na
heur passirt; ach, welch ein Schreck, dem Hau-se ganz nah, im Gar-ten die That ge-

Na
schah: Ninon. Ein Zweikampf war's! Deutlich sah Degen ich blitzen im Mondenschein!
Was sahst du da?
Mein Hil-fe-schrei'n rief Po-li-zei zwar schnell her-bei, doch ach, zu spät.
Ni
Himmel! Wie, zu
Der Ei-ne lag am Bo-den schon. Ja verwundet! Doch war sein Gegner bereits ent-
N
spät? Al-so ver-wundet?
Ninon, Gaston.
flohn! Wie Gegen des Kö-nigs strenges Verbot? Den Thäter die schwerste Stra-fe bedroht.
Fr. m. T. I.
Hö. m. T. II.
Wie Gegen des Kö-nigs strenges Verbot? Den Thäter die schwerste Stra-fe bedroht.
Chor.
La B. m. B.
cresc.
ff

Commissär
Halt Niemand von der Stelle! Man halte die Thüren besetzt!
Marsillac.
Hec_tor!
Hector (hinkend)
On_kel!
Più lento.
H
Ich!
Ja, ich hab ei_nen klei_nen Stich!
Hier in der
M
Du?
Du bist ver_wun_det?
Und wo?
Marsillac.
Hector (kläglich)
Hüf_te!
O Gott, wie lä_cherlich!
's ist un_ver_antwortlich;
mit mei_nen
Stich liess mich mein Gegner dort im Stich; und der leiden_de Theil bin ich!
stacc.
Dialog:

(Dadurch werden wir ihn entdecken.)
Poco meno mosso.
rall.
p
Ninon (leise)
Wird es ent-deckt, ist er ver-lo-ren!
Aubigné (leise)
Nur un-be-sorgt! Das Glück ist mir
Nanon.
Wä-re nur erst mein Grig-nan
Marsillac.
treu! Du bist zum Un-glück doch ge-bo-ren!
Hector.
Più lento.
frei! Ach, die Wun-de ist nicht ge-fähr-lich, nur das Ge-hen et-was be-
schwerlich!
Gaston. Nanon.
Ninon.
Frontenac.
Houlière.
In die Hüf-te ein Stich, wie be-dau-er-lich! Ha ha ha ha ha
Allegro.
rall.
f
p

ha!
ha!
ha ha ha ha ha ha!
ha ha ha ha ha ha!
Tempo di Valse.
Ninon.
Beim er - sten Mal wo er sich ge - schla - gen, beim er - sten Mal.
pp
Ni
wo ihm der Hel - den - ruhm winkt, hat er den Stich da - von nun ge -
Ni
tra - gen, der ar - me Vi - com - te er hinkt, er hinkt!
Ninon u. Ninon.
Ach, der ar - me Vi - comte er hinkt, er hinkt! Ach der ar - me Vi -

Gaston. Nanon. Ninon.
Ni
Na
comte er hinkt er hinkt Ach seht wie er hinkt, seht, wie er
Fronteme col Sopr. I.
Houlières col Sopr. II.
Ach seht wie er hinkt, seht, wie er
Aubigne col Tenor I
La Platre col Basso.
Chor.
mf
G
hinkt! Seht, wie er hinkt! Ach, seht wie er hinkt, seht wie er hinkt!
hinkt! Seht, wie er hinkt! Ach, seht wie er hinkt, seht wie er hinkt!
wie er
Seht, wie er hinkt, ha ha ha!
Seht, wie er hinkt, ha ha ha! Marsillac.
hinkt, In die Hü Hü Hüf. te ein Stich! Es ist nicht zu sagen! Die
p
p

Hector.
pp
f
Ja es war, (au) in der
kannst du lei-der ja nicht in der Schlinge tra-gen!
tr
pp
That äusserst in (au) de-li-cat!
In die Hü- fte ein
In die Hü- fte ein Stich!
rall.
a tempo.
Stich! Und jetzt werd' ich noch lä-cher-lich! Beim er-sten Mal wo
pp
ich mich ge-schlagen, beim er-sten Mal wo mir der Hel-denruhm winkt, hab ich den
Gaston. Nanon. Ninon.
Der ar-me Vi- comte er hinkt er hinkt!
Stich da- von nun ge-tra-gen!
cresc.

G
Na
Ni
Ach der ar_me Vi_comte, er hinkt, er hinkt! Ach, der arme Vi_comte er hinkt, er hinkt!
Frontenac.
Houlieres.
Ach der ar_me Vi_comte, er hinkt, er hinkt! Ach, der arme Vi_comte er hinkt, er hinkt!
Aubigné.
Ach der ar_me Vi_comte, er hinkt, er hinkt! Ach, der arme Vi_comte er hinkt, er hinkt!
Hector.
Ja der ar_mer Vi_comte, er hinkt, er hinkt! Ja, mein armer Vi_comte er hinkt, er hinkt!
Marsillac.
Ach der ar_me Vi_comte, er hinkt, er hinkt! Ach, der arme Vi_comte er hinkt, er hinkt!
La Platre.
Ach der ar_me Vi_comte, er hinkt, er hinkt! Ach, der arme Vi_comte er hinkt, er hinkt!
p
fz
fz
p
fz
fz
G
Na
Ni
Ach seht wie er hinkt, seht wie er hinkt seht wie er hinkt, Ach
F
Ho
Ach seht wie er hinkt, seht wie er hinkt seht wie er hinkt, Ach
A
Ach seht wie er hinkt, ja ja er hinkt ach ja er hinkt, Ach
He
Ach ja, ja er hinkt, ja ja er hinkt ach ja er hinkt, Ach
M
Ach ja, ja er hinkt, seht wie er hinkt seht wie er hinkt, Ach
Pl
Ach seht wie er hinkt, seht wie er hinkt seht wie er hinkt, Ach
Chor.
Ach wie er hinkt seht wie er hinkt seht wie er hinkt, Ach
ff
mf
ff

G
Na
Ni
seht wie er hinkt, seht wie er hinkt seht er hinkt
F
Ho
seht wie er hinkt, seht wie er hinkt seht er hinkt
A
seht wie er hinkt, seht wie er hinkt seht er hinkt
He
ach ja er hinkt, ach ja er hinkt ja Ach
M
seht wie er hinkt, seht wie er hinkt seht er hinkt
Pl
seht wie er hinkt, seht wie er hinkt seht er hinkt
seht wie er hinkt. seht wie er hinkt seht er hinkt
seht er hinkt

Gaston.
Nanon.
G
Na
Ni
er hinkt er hinkt er hinkt ach der ar_me Vi_ comt.
Ach
F
Ho
er hinkt er hinkt er hinkt ach der ar_me Vi_ comt.
Ach
A
er hinkt er hinkt er hinkt Ach
Ach der arme Vi_
He
ja ach ja Ach
Ja der arme Vi_
M
er hinkt er hinkt er hinkt Ach
Ach der arme Vi_ comt,
Pl
er hinkt er hinkt er hinkt Ach
Ach der arme Vi_ comt,
er hinkt er hinkt er hinkt ach der ar_me Vi_ comt,
Ach
er hinkt er hinkt er hinkt Ach
Ach der arme Vi_comt, ach der ar_me Vi_
er

G
Na
Ach er hinkt, er hinkt, er hinkt, er hinkt, er hinkt!
F
Ho
Ach er hinkt, er hinkt, er hinkt, er hinkt, er hinkt!
A
Ach er hinkt, er hinkt, er hinkt, er hinkt, er hinkt!
H
Ach er hinkt, er hinkt, er hinkt, er hinkt, er hinkt!
M
ach der arme Vi_comte, er hinkt, er hinkt, er hinkt, er hinkt, er hinkt!
Pl
ach der arme Vi_comte, er hinkt, er hinkt, er hinkt, er hinkt, er hinkt!
Ach er hinkt, er hinkt, er hinkt, er hinkt, er hinkt!
hinkt, ach der armen Vi_comte, er
acceler.

№ 15. Introduction.

strafenden Blick der Marquise salbungsvoll.)
rall.
An_na Dir sing ich mein Le_belang! Ja mein Le_be_lang!
Tempo I.
mf
p
Nº 16. Couplets.
Allegretto moderato
(scheinheilig.)
Marsillac.
Piano.
mf
p
Wenn ich auch Phi_lo_soph bin,
Einst jagt ich mehr wie bil_lig
blieb ich doch fro_mer Christ: hab man_chen Ju_gend_leichtsinn
welt_li_chen Freu_den nach, heut ist der Geist zwar wil_lig,
(ironisch seufzend.)
(lüstern.)
nicht oh_ne Reu' ge_büsst! Fühl' ich auch heut noch zärt_li_che Trie_be,
a_ber das Fleisch ist schwach! Mit Bal_le_ri_nen that ich sou_pi_ren,

mf (salbungsvoll.)
leb' ich nach dem Ge _ bot da _ rum: die all _ ge _ mei _ ne Men _ schen _ lie _ be
schenkt ih _ nen Ro _ ben gross _ muthsvoll, weil Hun _ gern _ de man soll trac _ ti _ ren,
Tempo di Valse.
üb' ich am In _ di _ vi _ du _ um.
und Decol'_ tir _ te klei _ den soll.
Der Wei _ se _ ste der Wei _ sen ist, wer
pp
molto cresc.
(mit voller Stimme.)
zeit _ wei _ se die gan _ ze Weis _ heit ver _ gisst! Der Wei _ se _ ste der
mf
Wei _ sen ist, wer zeit _ wei _ se die gan _ ze Weis _ heit ver _ gisst!
p
f
G.P.

Nº 17. Terzett.

A
Mein Herr ich fin.de das per - fid, pfui! das ist per.
M
Herr, ich fin.de das per - fid, ich fin.de das per - fid, pfui! das ist per.
Pl
fid! Da- ist per - fid, das ist per. fid, pfui! Das ist per.
sf
fz
p
fid, pfui, das ist per. fid! pfui! Wie
fid, pfui, das ist per. fid! pfui! Wie kommen Sie zu mei.nem
fid, pfui, das ist per. fid! pfui! Wie kommen Sie zu mei.nem Lied, wie kommen Sie zu
f
mf
kommen Sie zu mei.nem Lied? Ja, das ist mein Lied, ja das ist mein Lied! Ja!
Lied, ja zu mei.nem Lied, ja, das ist mein Lied, ja das ist mein Lied! Ja!
mei.nem Lied, zu mei.nem Lied, ja, da. ist mein Lied, ja das ist mein Lied! Ja!

A
M
Pl
Ja, das ist mein Min_ne_lied!
Das wär' Ihr Lied?
Das wär' Ihr Lied?
(f. s.)
Nur nicht ti_
p
(f. s.)
Mein Ei_genthum, in mei_ner Phan_ta_sie erblüht.
Nur nicht timid!
Sie bringen
mid!
Aubigné
mich in Miss_credit!
Er_fin_den Sie sich selbst ein Lied, dies ist von
Sie bringen mich in Miss_credit!
più lento
mir, dies ist von mir, dies ist von mir!
Nein, nein von mir, dies ist von mir!
Nein, nein von mir, dies ist von mir!
Ihr Herrn be_den_ket, wo Ihr seid! Ver_ständ'gen
f
più lento.
p

Pl
rallent.
wir uns oh_ne Streit! Sprecht doch mit Ruh und deut_lich_keit!
Aubigne.
Ganz deut_lich
rallent.
A
dehn und un_ver_ho_len, dies Lied, man hat es mir ge_stoh_len!
Marsillac.
Sie sind kurz an_ge_
M
bunden; ich hab's nur nah em_pfunden!
La Plâtre.
più lento.
Und ich, wie schon er_wähnet, ich hab es nur ent_ leh_net.
Allegretto.
Pl
Versprechen Sie, discret zu sein nun so gesteh ichs Ihnen ein, ich hört es gestern v. Mar_
quis, der es bei Ninon sang.
Aubigné.
Wie, Sie?
Marsillac.
Wie kamen Sie da_zu?
Pl
Ja ich!
Ge_stehen

M
will ich en_tre_nous, bei Na_non hört' ich heimlich zu; mit sehr vernehmlichem Te_
Aubigné (verlegen.)
M
nor sang es ihr dort ein Tambour vor.
Ein Tambour bei Na_non?
Zu die_nen!
La Plâtre. (zu Aubigne.)
So ist es al_so
Marsillac.
Un_mög_lich! Wie wär's zu er_klä_ren, dass ich's bei Na_non konn_te
Pl
nicht von Ih_nen?
M
hö_ren? Ge_stehn Sie denn auch uns geschwind, wie Sie da_zu ge_kommen sind?
Aub. (f.s.)
Was
Pl
Ge_stehn Sie denn auch uns geschwind, wie Sie da_zu ge_kommen sind?
A
sag ich nur?
(laut.)
Nun, der Tam_bour, der Tam_bour, den bei Na_non Sie ge_

A
M
Pl
hört, der-sel-be hats auch mich ge-lehrt. Ja der Tam-bour!
Der Tam-bour? (ungläubig.) Hm.
(ungläubig.)
Der Tam-bour? Hm,
hm hm hm hm hm! wär hät-te das ge-dacht, ein Tambour hat dies
hm hm hm hm hm! wär hät-te das ge-dacht, ein Tambour hat dies
Lied ge-macht? Mu-sik wie Dichtung zart und fein, der Tam-bour muss ta-
Lied ge-macht? Mu-sik wie Dichtung zart und fein, der Tam-bour muss ta-
Aubigne (f.s.)
lent-voll sein! Dass sel - ber ich dies Lied er-
lent-voll sein! Ein Tam-bour, tam, tam, tam ra-ta plan, plan, plan, plan,

A
M
Pl
dacht nehm' zu gestehn ich mich in Acht; sonst wär
Ein Tam_bour, tam, tam, tam, ra_ta plan plan plan plan plan ra_ta plan plan plan plan
plan! ra_ta plan plan plan plan
so_fort es of_fen_bar, wer bei Na_non als Tam_bour war.
plan, ra_ta plan plan plan plan plan ra_ta plan plan plan plan plan plan plan. Der
plan, ra_ta plan plan plan plan plan ra_ta plan plan plan plan plan plan plan. Der
Ja der ist ei_ne wah_re Perl, ra_ta plan plan plan!
Tambour scheint ein Teufels_kerl, ra_ta plan plan plan!
Tambour scheint ein Teufels_kerl, ra_ta plan plan plan! So
Ein Dieb? Das ist schlecht aus_ge_drückt, Man darf bei
wa_ren Sie der er_ste Dieb?

Allegro non troppo.
geist'gem Mein und Dein gar so difficil nicht sein! Nein
Aubig. I. St.
Zwar Diebstahl ist ein schwer Ver_gehen, die Uhr ab_zwi_cken Schand'und Sünd! Ge_
La Pl. II. St.
Der Com_po_nist so wie der Dichter, weiss sel_ten sel_ber was er singt. Drum
Mars. III. St.
Der Au_tor ist ein schlech_ter Kenner von dem, was gra_de zün_det oft. Ge_
pp
A
dan_ken schni_pfen, das mag ge_hen, weil ja Ge_dan_ken zoll_frei sind; wenn
Pl
sei man nicht zu stren_ger Rich_ter, wenn er's nur bo_na_fi_de bringt; wenn
M
Pe_ga_sus, der ed_le Rei_mer, macht Sei_ten_sprün_ge un_ver_hofft: Was
A
das Ge_dächt_niss uns so treu ist, das Al_les man behält was neu ist, so
Pl
er, vom Ge_nius in_spi_ri_ret, in's Reich der Phanta_sie ge_füh_ret hört
M
man in wei_he_vol_len Stun_den mit Schmerz ge_bo_ren tief em_pfunden, für

weiss man selbst oft nicht zu sa_gen, obs Ei_gen_thum, obs nur ent_tra_gen? Und
sü_sse Zau_ber_wei_sen schal_len, die An_dern frü_her ein_ge_fal_len, ist
gött_lich hielt, für aus_er_le_sen, das war schon öf_ter da_ge_we_sen; wer
rall.
a tempo.
Eins steht fest ganz si_cher_lich! Schö_ne Geister begeg_nen sich, die begeg_nen
Er da_für ver_ant_wort_lich! Schö_ne Geister begeg_nen sich, die begeg_nen
ist da_für ver_ant_wort_lich! Schö_ne Geister begeg_nen sich, die begeg_nen
1, 2.
sich! Schö_ne Gei_ster begeg_nen sich, die be_geg_nen sich!
sich! Schö_ne Gei_ster begeg_nen sich, die be_geg_nen sich!
sich! Schö_ne Gei_ster begeg_nen sich, die be_geg_nen sich!
Schluss.
sich!
sich!
sich!

Nº 18. Couplets.

ko - ket - tirt und Kü - sse schickt, wie man seufzt und
drü - cke zu die Äu - ge - lein, wenn es wirk - lich
mf
Hän - de drückt bei ver - lieb - ten Ne - cke - rei'n;
müss - te sein, hielt auch still dann oh - ne Schrei'n;
Più animato.
pp
Doch wo - zu? 's muss ja nicht sein, je - doch wo -
zu? 's muss ja nicht sein, 's muss ja nicht sein, 's muss ja nicht
leggiero.
p
f
a piacere.
sein, nein, nein, nein, 's muss ja nicht sein!

Nº 19. Schluss.

f
Nanon.
Schon war ernstlich uns bang, so bang, so bang Nun klingt fröhlich der Sang, der Sang, der Sang
Ninon.
Gaston.
Schon war ernstlich uns bang, so bang, so bang Nun klingt fröhlich der Sang, der Sang, der Sang
Front.
Houl.
Arm.
Schon war ernstlich uns bang, so bang, so bang Nun klingt fröhlich der Sang, der Sang, der Sang
Aubigné
Hector.
Schon war ernstlich uns bang, so bang, so bang Nun klingt fröhlich der Sang, der Sang, der Sang
Mars.
Schon war ernstlich uns bang, so bang, so bang Nun klingt fröhlich der Sang, der Sang, der Sang
Abbe.
Schon war ernstlich uns bang, so bang, so bang Nun klingt fröhlich der Sang, der Sang, der Sang
p
N
Ach Fröh - li - cher Sang, fröh - li - cher Sang, fröh - li - cher
Ni
G
Ach Fröh - li - cher Sang, fröh - li - cher Sang, fröh - li - cher
F
H
A
Ach Fröh - li - cher Sang, fröh - li - cher Sang, fröh - li - cher
Au
He
Ach Fröh - li - cher Sang, fröh - li - cher Sang, fröh - li - cher
M
Ach Fröh - li - cher Sang, fröh - li - cher Sang, fröh - li - cher
P
Ach Fröh - li - cher Sang, fröh - li - cher Sang, fröh - li - cher
Ach Fröh - li - cher Sang, fröh - li - cher Sang, fröh - li - cher

ff
Sang, ja fröh - li-cher Sang, fröh - li-cher Sang
ff
Sang, ja fröh - li-cher Sang, fröh - li-cher Sang
ff
Sang, ja fröh - li-cher Sang, fröh - li-cher Sang
ff
Sang, ja fröh - li-cher Sang, fröh - li-cher Sang
ff
Sang, ja fröh - li-cher Sang, fröh - li-cher Sang
ff
Sang, ja fröh - li-cher Sang, fröh - li-cher Sang
ff
Sang, ja fröh - li-cher Sang, fröh - li-cher Sang
ff
ff

noch
lang der Sang, noch lang der Sang, noch lang!
noch
noch
noch
noch
noch
noch
accel.
ENDE.

PLEASURE'S WAND.

"We Obey no Wand but Pleasure's."—*Tom Moore*.

A crowded and fashionable audience assembled at the Baldwin on Monday evening to see and hear what is claimed to be the genuine *Nanon*, with Genee's music and Sydney Rosenfeld's translation of Zell's libretto, and produced by the Carleton Opera Company, with Professor J. Hiller, K. S., R. A. M., as conductor. The still unfinished litigation here, over the exclusive right to produce the opera, and the five performances of it —September 7th, 16th and 17th, and October 19th and 20th—at the Tivoli, had whetted, rather than satiated, the public eagerness for this long-promised treat, and in compliance with the request of the management, nearly every seat was occupied by eight o'clock. Nevertheless the audience was a little reserved, and even the favorite Carleton was less warmly welcomed than he had a right to expect, while Miss Louise Paullin, Mr. C. H. Drew (perhaps not generally recognized at first) and Miss Clara Wisdom received but scanty applause as they successively appeared. And throughout the performance, although there were frequent encores, there was no real enthusiasm; the feeling was rather that of disappointment, while, nevertheless, there seemed little ground for hostile criticism. Something startling was looked for, and something very mild was found. The whole performance seemed to lack force and incisiveness. But a second hearing of the opera happily reassured us. The company was seen to be thoroughly balanced, and trained to produce an *ensemble* almost faultless; indeed, we recall nothing here which has so nearly approached the French methods as the groupings, the demeanor and the dialogue of the subordinate performers in *Nanon*. With Seabury's beautiful scenery, and the fresh and elegant costumes, the performance is a succession of delightful stage pictures. Such a picture is that on which the curtain rises, and another is the finale of the second act, which is always redemanded. In short, the strength of the company is in its harmonious co-operation, and, if for nothing but this, its performances may be heard with constantly increasing pleasure.

* * * * *

Mr. Carleton is unquestionably the best singer in the company, and although the transpositions and avoidances which he finds necessary are certainly detrimental to the brightness of his tenor role of D'Aubigné, yet he is in every other respect so admirable as to remain the undisputed favorite of the cast. His interpolated introductory song, a graceful thing in 6 8 time, is always encored, and so, of course, is the waltz, both when sung to Nanon in the first act and to Ninon in the second. Miss Louise Paullin has worn off some of her primness during the past five years, and makes a charming Nanon, giving full effect to the music, and acting with equal spirit and refinement. Miss Alice Vincent, a tall and handsome blonde, and a fair singer, is a fascinating Ninon de l' Enclos (or, as Drew calls her, with a pun which falls unheeded, "Ninon in long clothes"); a little care would prevent her from saying "ben" for "been," "feet for "fête," and "Henrée" for "Henri." Miss Clara Wisdom, as tall and as beautiful as before, doubles the part of Mme. De Maintenon with that of Bombardini. Miss Josephine Bartlett, with a pleasant face and very graceful figure, plays Gaston, the page to Ninon, and the phrase or two in which her pleasant singing voice is heard by itself makes us wish that her song in the second act had not been cut out. Mr. Drew, always a favorite here, has aged somewhat since his last visit, and his singing voice has no great value, but he is a most vivacious actor, and gives much life to all his scenes; indeed, he is sometimes too obstreperous, and would do well to bring his role of De Marsillac into more quiet relation to the rest. He wins a nightly encore for his "impressario" song, and for his abortive rendering of the waltz, this latter scene, by the way, with the group of ladies and courtiers, and the twelve pretty violinists and flutists who accompany his song, being one of the most enjoyable things in the opera. Mr. C. M. Leumane, who appears as Hector, has a nice tenor voice and an agreeable manner. He interpolates a song, "It's only a question of time," which, on the first night, contained a verse, in rather bad taste, about the pending litigation; on Wednesday he did not get far enough to introduce it. Mr. Joseph M. Greensfelder (or Mr. H. Ehrend—the stupid programme leaves us in doubt) doubles the role of Pierre, which he sings in Anglo-Dutch, with that of the Abbe, and, in the third act, displays immense lung capacity in the prolonged notes of the devotional version of the waltz, with organ accompaniment, in which he is regularly encored. Another encore in this scene is for Drew's couplets, to which the roguish behavior of the two nuns and their lapse into actual waltzing during the delicious eight measures for the orchestra, contribute no little of its success. Mr. Tom Guise doubles the part of King Louis XIV with that of the Corporal—the latter not named. These omissions and errors in a house programme are silly and irritating; there are three of them in this.

* * * * *

We have heard a great deal about the costumes of the New York *Nanon*, and, although no scientific description of them has reached us, yet we have been led to expect that the twelve handsome drummers and fifers of the first act, who reappear as violinists and flutists in the second, and contribute their presence to the finale of the third, would be almost absolutely unclothed. But all such apprehensions were promptly removed. In deference no doubt to the superior modesty of San Francisco audiences, the New York costumes were not literally copied, and those which are worn here are far less daring than have often been seen on our stage.

* * * * *

New National Theatre.

W. H. RAPLEY .... MANAGER

Washington Second Week of

Summer Opera

—BY THE—

Fitz-Gerald Opera Co.,

COMMENCING MONDAY EVEN'G, JUNE 13th,
SATURDAY MATINEE, 187

GENEE'S CHARMING OPERA IN THREE ACTS

—NANON—

CAST OF CHARACTERS.

Nanon Patin, Hostess of the Golden Lamb..	Miss Clara Lane
Ninon de L'enclos................	Miss Helen Von Donhoff
Maintenon...........................	Miss Jennie Reifferth
Gaston, Page of Ninon.............	Miss Marie Greenwood
Marquis de Aubinge................	Mr. Wm. F. Pruette
Marquis de Marsillac................	Mr. Harry Standish
Abbe....................................	Mr. Joseph S. Greensfelder
Hector, Nephew of Marsillac..........	Mr. Edward Gervaise
Corporal	Mr. Renwick
Mme. de Frontenac..................	Miss Minnie Galloway
Countesse Houlliers..................	Miss Effie Wilton
Jacqueline	Miss Kitty Greene
Therese, Aunt of Nanon..............	Miss Grace Caldwell
Lisette..................................	Miss Annie Haines
Cousin Pierre..........................	Mr. Fred'k DeLeon
Cousin Joan	Mr. S. C. Porter
Uncle Mathew..........................	Mr. T. J. Bryant
Bombadini..............................	Mr. Sydney Durham
Sergeant...............................	Mr. Geo. A. Smyth
Notary.................................	Mr. W. D. Morris
Baptiste, Page to Mlle. de Maintenon.	Miss Florence Sinclair
First Lady in Waiting................	Miss Lillie Hawthorne
Second Lady in Waiting.............	Miss Ellen Hawthorne
King Louis XIV.........................	Mr. Farnum

STAGE DIRECTOR .... MR. JOSEPH S. GREENSFELDER
MUSICAL DIRECTOR .... MR. MAX HIRSCHFELD

GRAND OPERA HOUS

Opera in English.

1898

NANON," vivacious, clear and gay with refined French gayety, was given at the American ...eatre Monday evening. A series of beautiful stage pic...es was presented, showing the ample resources of the ...mpany in the way of good looks, costumes and stage ...operties in general. There were constant evidences ...roughout the opera that the stage management is far ...perior to that which usually controls the productions of ...ese light operas. It is only by the careful attention to ...tail of color and grouping that such excellent results ...n be attained. Little fault could be found with the act...g, for added familiarity with the lines will remove the ...ght uncertainty of a first night performance. The sing...g was characteried by spontaneity and refined humor. The libretto has a certain historic interest. The action ...es place in the days of Louis Quatorze, Madame de ...aintenon and Ninon de l'Enclos, and the Marquis de ...arsellac, a gentleman who varied his court duties by an ...erest in the stage. He considers himself a comedian

than in ... de Ma... The ... ing so... "make... dience. for m... presen... offered ... The co...

Marqu... Hector... Marqu... Bomba... Louis... Mons. The N... Ninon... Madam... Counte... Gaston... Mme. ... Cousin... Uncle... Papa ... Cousin... Mothe... Aunt ... Cousin... Jacque... Sergea... Ch...

In l... an env... ent: h... makes... class o... of dee... bilities... Oscar... that h... On ...

Donnerstag, den 9. August,

NANON!

Die Wirthin vom Goldenen Lamm.

Operette in 3 Akten von Richard Genee.

König Ludwig XIV	OTTO MEYER
Frau von Maintenon	RUSCHA MICHAELIS
Marquis d'Aubigne, ihr Neffe...	FERDINAND SCHUETZ
Ninon de L'Enclos........................	JENNY BOUER
Frau von Frontenac, } Ninon's	MARIE SCHLAG
Gräfin Houlieres, } Freundinnen .	VERA HERRNKOHL
Marquis von Marsillac, Intendant der königlichen Schauspiele...	MAX LUBE
Hector, Vicomte von Marsillac, sein Neffe.	RUD. SINNHOLD
Nanon Patin, Wirthin vom "Goldenen Lamm".	LORI STUBEL
Bertrand, }	EDUARD HIRSCH
Pierre, } deren Verwandte	EUGEN KUBACH
Jean, }	CONRAD BECK
Therese, }	ALBERTINE HABRICH
Abbe la Platre........................	BERNHARD RANK
Gaston, Ninon's Page	MARIE HARTMANN
Bombardini, Tambourmajor...	HUGO WICHERT
Baptiste, Diener bei Frau von Maintenon	HEINR. HABRICH
Ein Sergeant........................	FRANZ v. METSCH
Ein Corporal	HERMAN GEROLD

Festgäste, Offiziere, Soldaten, Herren und Damen von Hofe.

Die Handlung spielt in Paris, um's Jahr 1685. Der erste Akt in Nanon's Wirthshause; der zweite bei Ninon de L'Enclos; der dritte bei Frau von Maintenon.

In the Second Act Appearance of the

GYPSY MARIONETTES

Im 2. Akt, Auftreten der Zigeuner-Marionetten.

Das ungarische Prinzenpaar und die lebenden Zigeuner-Marionetten:

Aranka Salzer. Senor Salzer.

Maghar Toncosak.

Freitag und Sonnabend... .... **Mad. Angot**
Sonntag, den 12. August............ **Extra Concert**

reliable members of the Castle Square Company. He learns his dialogue with astonishing rapidity, and his music almost entirely by ear. Yet, it will be noted by those who listen carefully that his intonation is true, and that he is as much at home in the music as in the words of his part. His quickness is no doubt partly due to the French strain in his ancestry. He is of good French family through his mother, a clever and accomplished woman, who has more than ordinary musical ability.

An example of his intellectuality worth noting is the playing of twenty operas in twelve weeks during his first

her voice and by her beauty. Harold Bauer played Chopin in his remarkable manner, and Madame de Reibna sang superbly. She and her father, Mr. Schlesinger, have left for the season at Nice.

PIANO MUSIC FOR VERY YOUNG PUPILS.

At the concert of the Beethoven Normal School of Piano were played the following compositions by children, from seven to fourteen possibly. As each piece had been chosen for some special object in piano education, and as all of them were interesting, some of them very pretty, perhaps the list may be useful to some teachers of piano. By Beethoven, Menuet of the Eighteenth Sonata and finale of the First Symphony for eight hands; by Mozart, an Andante; by Mendelssohn, Caprice in E minor; Schumann, "Elévation," from "Pieces Romantique"; Wagner-Liszt, "Spinning Song," from "Flying Dutchman"; Chopin, Scherzo in B flat minor, Impromptu in F major, Valse in A minor, Polonaise in C sharp minor; Weber, Larghetti and Allegro Passionato of Concertstück: Guilmant

Wagner lore has existed all the season. Yet a few, ve... few years ago, Wagner was carried in rag effigy throu... the streets here, "conspued," "à bas" ed and "à l'eau" d... the street mob to the street mob's content. And wh... asked why they did so, and who the culpable was a... what he had done to merit the treatment, they repl... that they did not know and they did not care. It w... something to "conspuer," something to make "a cav... cade." It was a—"fête"!

The "l'Or du Rhin" was a strange performance. F... gods, three goddesses, three daughters of the Rhine, t... Nibelungen and two giants began their "hard wo... when people had scarcely risen from their dinner tab... throughout the city. They were still barking and howl... and yelping away there after the people had all disper... in carriages and omnibuses over the city at midnig... As there was no stop or break to the continuance the p... ple who came late were obliged to slip and slide in m... any-way, contrary to the discipline of most conce... which prevents entrance during the "execution" of ... piece. As there was but one "piece," and it was all "e... cution," they were obliged to be let in. This movem... had scarcely ceased when those within began to l... about for means of escape. As there was evidently ... chance of an entr'acte they began slipping and sliding

Castle Square Theatre—"Nanon"

[illegible] comic operetta, "Nanon," was the attraction at the Castle Square Theatre last evening, the principal characters being distributed as follows:

Marquis de Marsillac	Mr. Oscar Girard
[illegible] de Marsillac	Mr. Edward [illegible]
Marquis [illegible] d'Aubigné	Mr. J. K. Murray
[illegible]	Mr. W. H. Clarke
[illegible]	Miss Clara Lane
[illegible]	Miss Laura Millard
[illegible] de Maintenon	Miss Rose Leighton

Despite the fact that the familiar love song of D'Aubigné and Nanon in the opening act permeates the whole score and is forever recurring as the paramount feature in the music, it cannot be said that it is the only music in the operetta. On the contrary, the score contains many other real gems; it is pleasantly and artistically varied, and both in the recitative and the lyrical parts there is a deal of excellent musical humor. The sandwiching of the love song into the cantata in the third act, for instance, is especially droll. The libretto of "Nanon" is far superior to the average comic operetta book, and in last night's performance there was no attempt to ruin it by the intrusion of alien absurdities. It is only a waste of words to say that the performance was exceedingly meritorious, for the Castle Square Theatre has won a reputation which precludes the necessity of any such statement.

We have already hinted that the performance last evening was an exceedingly good one, and so it was. There were, it is true, occasional panderings to the groundlings, but why should not the groundlings be considered as well as the judicious? They pay as much for their seats and some there are who maintain, alas! that they are in the majority. However this may be, it must be admitted, even by the ultra-judicious, that in "Nanon" the groundlings are but scantily fed, and that in the main the actors endeavor to be true to their art, and that they generally succeed in their endeavors.

Miss Clara Lane was at her very best, both in acting and singing; the only fault that can be brought against her (and that may have been the fault of the stage director) was that there was something too much of her repetition of the formula as to the sweetness of her Grignan. Lightning, it is said, strikes but once in the same place; and a "cute" saying is only bright when it is first heard; by repetition it soon becomes silly and nauseating. Miss Lane is a dainty, a delicacy, in her own words, "too sweet for anything," and it is therefore too bad to blemish her work—and the brighter the object the more obvious the blemish—by the needless and exasperating repetition of the formula referred to. In thus speaking we are aware that we run counter to the opinion of some eminent playwrights, who conceive that only in repetitious composition is to be found true humor and real wit. All of the other principals were good and some of them excellent; and particular credit is due to Mr. Murray, Mr. Clarke, Mr. Girard, Miss Millard and Miss Leighton. The chorus did grandly and the orchestra, under the baton of Mr. Hirschfeld, performed its work in a musicianly manner.

SEPTEMBER 2[illegible], 1889.

"NANON" AT BIRMINGHAM.

A Comic Opera, Written and Composed by Richard Genée, Played for the First Time in England at the Grand Theatre, Birmingham, on Monday, Sept. 16th, 1889.

Nanon Patin	Miss Laura Clement
Madame Maintenon	Miss Annie Brophy
Gaston	Miss Marie Wenter
Jacqueline	Miss Ruby West
Mdlle. Frontenac	Miss Kate Bellingham
Mdlle. Hunlieres	Miss Louise Franklyn
Therese	Miss Rose Benton
Lisette	Miss Beatrice Fubbela
Page to Madame Maintenon	Miss Winifred Gordon
Marquis D'Aubigny	Mr Deane Brand
Marsillac	Mr W. H. Rawlins
Hector	Mr Gilbert Porteous
Abbé	Mr Allen Morris
Pierre	Mr Charles Bernie
Sergeant	Mr Finn
Commissioner	Mr Richardson
Notary	Mr Allen
King Louis XIV	Mr Sam Finney
Ninon	Miss Esme Lee

(FROM OUR OWN CORRESPONDENT.)

Hardly had the echo of the applause t[illegible] *Ruy Blas* died away ere another new piec[e was sub]mitted to the patrons of the Grand Theat[re, in a] succession of novelties probably unequall[ed in] recollection. *Nanon* is new, and yet [not] new, for in America it had become quite [a] favourite. At the Casino Theatre, New Y[ork, it] played five hundred times, and then [i]t for 1,500 nights. English playgoers will only [have a] comic opera to which they have yielded a measure of popularity. Whether they [will allow] *Nanon* to depose *Les Cloches de Corneville* [from the] proud position that it now holds in the re[pertory of the] stage remains to be seen. We doubt it. *Na[non* is] called a comic opera only by somewhat arbit[rary classi]fication. The dialogue is not characterised by any desperate attempt at wit; nor has the author been liberal in affording opportunities to his comedians. If, as time goes on, they deliberately justify their existence, the opera may gain in popularity. *Nanon* is, in fact, a romantic opera—neither deep enough in its passion, nor sufficiently exalted in its musical aims to be called grand; of the respectable middle class, to speak plainly, in style, sentiment, and surroundings. There is a neatly trimmed plot, told in an elegant and grammatical way, to a musical accompaniment of pretty melodies that neither strike one by much originality, nor any artistic *gaucherie*.

The scene is laid in France, in the picturesque period of the Grand Monarque, who, in an incidental way, figures in the piece. Nanon is the hostess of the Golden Lamb, a hostelry made famous in the beginning by a chance visit of the king, and kept popular by the sprightly wit and other charms of Nanon. The pretty creature has admirers by the battalion—rich and rustic. She has set her heart on one who calls himself Sergeant Grignon, for the simple reason that he is the Marquis D'Aubigny. He chooses the highly original method of courting with a detachment of drummers in attendance. This robs the lovers of privacy, but comes in very handy for spectacular and musical effect. Nanon takes her admirer so completely at his word as to make every arrangement for their wedding—even invites the guests, and calls in the notary. D'Aubigny, indeed, looks in one day to find himself a most important factor in an ornate and elaborate ceremony, from which he escapes at a critical moment by getting himself arrested on a trivial charge of duelling. Nanon is distressed. But she recalls the fact that the great beauty of those times Ninon de l'Enclos had once promised to be her friend in any access of trouble, and so to Ninon she repairs, with the view of enlisting her sympathies in behalf of the poor prisoner. As a matter of fact, Sergeant Grignon, in his capacity of Marquis D'Aubigny, is the accepted lover of Ninon. Having escaped from prison by the simple expedient of walking out, D'Aubigny turns up at the court of the proud beauty, and explains his absence in a song. Nanon arrives, tells her short sad story, and easily enlists the sympathy of Ninon in behalf of her beloved, but perfidious, Grignon. Meanwhile that amorous tenor has got himself into real trouble, and when, in the third act, Nanon waits on Madame de Maintenon, with a view to getting Grignon pardoned by the King, Ninon has a similar favour to ask in behalf of her D'Aubigny. When in the end D'Aubigny's accumulation of indiscretions seems likely to lose his head for him, he owes his life and liberty to the captivating Nanon, who has even succeeded in fascinating the King. With half a mind to leave the deceitful creature to his fate, Nanon arrives at the more merciful decision to spare him, and the grateful D'Aubigny, thus brought to a full appreciation of her worth, makes her a Marquise.

To Miss Laura Clement the opera owes much of the success that it achieved on the night of its production. She is a bright, vivacious actress, and sings more than acceptably. The author has had the curious idea of giving his heroine a "wheeze" all to her own share, such as low comedians are wont to cultivate assiduously at Christmas time. "Ain't he sweet? Now ain't he sweet? Ain't he just too sweet for anything?" says Nanon, on the slightest provocation. If Miss Clement could obtain permission to utter this curious remark say five-and-twenty times fewer in the course of the evening, she would deserve the even more grateful recognition of audiences already deeply indebted to her. Ninon the beautiful finds an admirable representative in Miss Esme Lee, whose bad cold on Monday robbed her voice of the sweetness and strength that it is known to possess, but could not deprive her figure of grace nor her personality of interest. Mr Deane Brand is the D'Aubigny. He shows off various handsome costumes with effect, sings several solos excellently, and makes, indeed, a very acceptable hero. Mr Allen Morris as the Abbé only has the chance to sing one solo; but he does this in a manner that wins him quite a large share of the musical honours. Mr Sam Finney, the King Louis, and Miss Annie Brophy, the Madame de Maintenon, have very little to do, but acquit themselves with much credit. To Mr W. H. Rawlins and Mr Gilbert Porteous are entrusted the two important parts of Marsillac and Hector. These at present are mere outline sketches, but they have great potentialities. De Marsillac is a pompous old worldling, and Hector his extremely stupid nephew. The elder reprobate is bringing up the younger in the way of foppery and flirtation. Their deeds and dilemmas are the nearest approach to the comic in *Nanon*. If the author seek to win the suffrages of popular audiences he will do well to develop the "business" of these gentry. A heart-seeking sentimental ballad for the heroine and a smart topical song might work wonders. Such things no doubt detract a little from the artistic excellence of an opera, but they delight Demos in the pit. And why should not Demos be delighted? He, of course, pays the piper. Mr R. Redford is exploiting *Nanon*; and he has fitted her out for the tour with much artistic taste and liberality. The dresses, tempo Louis XIV., are extremely beautiful. The chorus is numerous and attractive.

"Nanon"—86th Street Garden

"NANON," a German screen operetta by Zell and Genee, music by Alois Melichar, directed by Herbert Maisch and presented by UFA at the Eighty-sixth Street Garden Theater with the following cast:

Nanon Patin	Erna Sack
Marquis Charles d'Aubigne	Johannes Heesters
Pierre	Berthold Ebbecke
Louis XIV	Karl Paryla
Ninon de l'Enclos	Dagny Servaes
Marquis de Marsillac	Oskar Sima
Hector	Kurt Meisel
Jean Baptiste Moliere	Otto Gebuehr
Die Tänzerin	Ursula Deinert
Francois Patin	Clemens Hasse
Mons. Louvois	Walter Steinbeck
Mons. Duval	Hermann Pfeiffer

"Nanon," the new German film operetta at the Garden Theater this week, is worthy of Hollywood. This UFA production, based upon a story by Zell and Genee, with music by Alois Melichar, is a pretentious undertaking, handsomely mounted and costumed. Nov 28, 1938 [illegible]

Nanon, a charming little innkeeper of the France of Louis XIV, is madly in love with Charles Grignan, who she believes is a soldier. He really is the Marquis d'Aubigne, in search of adventure and romance. Nanon has prepared a wedding feast in anticipation of Charles's arrival, inviting the townsfolk to attend. Panic-stricken, Charles pretends to be arrested for duelling and Nanon sets about to release him. After many sequences, with humorous complications, Nanon gets her man through a ruse by her friend, the playwright Moliere.

Erna Sack, one of Europe's leading coloratura sopranos, plays and sings the role of Nanon pleasantly. Johannes Heesters, who scored a success in "Bettelstudent," proves again that he is a fine singer and actor. Oskar Sima, Kurt Meisel and Otto Gebuehr also perform effectively.

E. G.